Il-2 Stormovik

By Hans-Heiri Stapfer
Color by Don Greer
Illustrated by Joe Sewell

in action

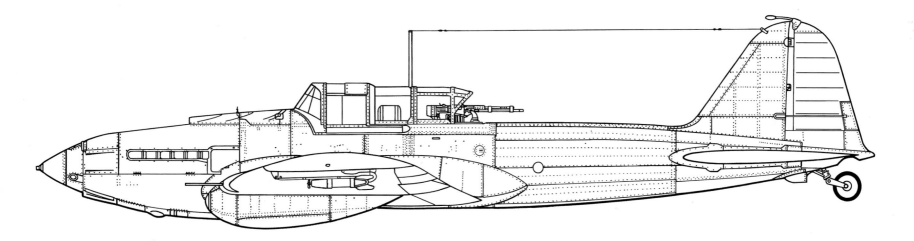

Aircraft Number 155

squadron/signal publications

A Il-2 Type 3 Stormovik attacks a German airfield with rockets and gun fire. The Il-2 was the best attack aircraft the Soviets had during the Great Patriotic War (the Second World War).

Acknowledgments

Viktor Kulikov	Robert Bock	Hannu Valtonen	Klaus Niska
Heinz J. Norarra	Dr. Volker Koos	Milan Micevski	Slava Sagoruiko
E.C.P.A. Paris	Odon Horvath	Hans-Joachim Mau	V. Simecek
Wolfgang Tamme	Jiri Vrany	Zdenek Titz	Dave Hatherell
Hadtorteneti Muzeum	Dusan Mikolas	Andrew Zinchuck	Dan Antoniu
Andras Nagy	Mihail Moisescu	Richard Forster	G.F. Petrov
Carl-Fredrik Geust	Steven Zaloga	Mariusz Konarski	Mariusz Zimny
A. A. Zirnov	Andrzej Morgala	Vladimir Gagin	Zdenek Klima
Larry Davis	Tibor Sinka	S.H.A.A. Paris	Keski-Suomen
Ilmailumuseo	Nigel A. Eastaway	George Punka	Attila Bonhardt
Ivo Zetik	Ivo Rusak	Zdenek Hurt	Mike Kirk
James V. Crow	Martin Dorsky	Bernard Denes	Renald Gravel
Jan Horn	Albert Violand	Manfred Griehl	Alain Pelletier
Martin Kyburz	Nigel A. Eastaway	Martin Villing	Peter Stache
Yefim Gordon	Roman Sekyrka	Stephan Boshniakov	Ivan Ivanov
Viktor K. Kabanov	Andrzej Ec	Thomas Heinicke	USAF Museum
Nicholas J. Waters III	Smithsonian Institution		

The Il-2 Stormovik was by far the most successful attack aircraft used by the Red Air Force on the Eastern Front during the Great Patriotic War. The Il-2 was produced in a number of variants and a total of 36,163 were produced during the war. This Il-2 Type 3, Yellow 12, has the tactical number repeated on the port wing tip. (G.F. Petrov)

ISBN 0-89747-341-8

If you have any photographs of aircraft, armor, soldiers or ships of any nation, particularly wartime snapshots, why not share them with us and help make Squadron/Signal's books all the more interesting and complete in the future. Any photograph sent to us will be copied and the original returned. The donor will be fully credited for any photos used. Please send them to:

Squadron/Signal Publications, Inc.
1115 Crowley Drive
Carrollton, TX 75011-5010

Если у вас есть фотографии самолётов, вооружения, солдат или кораблей любой страны, особенно, снимки времён войны, поделитесь с нами и помогите сделать новые книги издательства Эскадрон/Сигнал ещё интереснее. Мы переснимем ваши фотографии и вернём оригиналы. Имена приславших снимки будут сопровождать все опубликованные фотографии. Пожалуйста, присылайте фотографии по адресу:

Squadron/Signal Publications, Inc.
1115 Crowley Drive
Carrollton, TX 75011-5010

軍用機、装甲車両、兵士、軍艦などの写真を所持しておられる方はいらっしゃいませんか？どの国のものでも結構です。作戦中に撮影されたものが特に良いのです。Squadron/Signal社の出版する刊行物において、このような写真は内容を一層充実し、興味深くすることができます。当方にお送り頂いた写真は、複写の後お返しいたします。出版物中に写真を使用した場合は、必ず提供者のお名前を明記させて頂きます。お写真は下記にご送付ください。

Squadron/Signal Publications, Inc.
1115 Crowley Drive
Carrollton, TX 75011-5010

Author's Note

Soviet documents and literature reveal that no suffix designations were assigned by the manufacturer or the Soviet Air Force to identify single or two seat versions of the Stormovik. The aircraft were simply referred to as Il-2s. This was in sharp contrast to designation systems used in the west, where each new type or sub-variant of a new type automatically received an official designation for proper identification. The Soviets simply felt this system was unnecessary.

The designations Il-2M and Il-2 Type 3, which are found in Western literature, are unofficial designations and never officially used. In order to better understand the aircraft, these designations have been used in the "Il-2 Stormovik in action." Additionally, I have seen the name Stormovik spelled at least five different ways in various publications. For Stormovik in action, we will use the spelling, Stormovik throughout.

Introduction

In the Soviet Union a cumbersome, slow, but heavily armed and armored ground attack aircraft, which was unique in many respects, became one of the most decisive weapons in the inventory of the Red Army.

The Stormovik assault aircraft, as Sergej V. Ilyushin's Il-2 was generally called, proved to be exactly what the Red Army needed to support their ground forces against the invading Germans, from the Summer of 1941 to final victory in Berlin on 9 May 1945.

The Il-2 Stormovik was by far one of the most efficient weapons in the **Voyenno-Vozdushnyye Sily** (Red Air Force). The Stormovik soon became a nightmare for enemy tanks, motor vehicles, artillery and infantry. The Germans generally referred to the Il-2 as the **Schwarzer Tod** (Black Death). Il-2 pilots flew combat sorties at very low levels, flying at altitudes of between thirty and 6,000 feet, armed with a variety of weapons, including machine guns, cannon, bombs and rockets.

A dramatic wartime telegram from the Soviet dictator, Iosif Stalin, to the manufacturing plant, reflected the great importance this aircraft type had in his view. "The Red Army needs the Il-2 as it needs air and bread. I urge you to produce more Ilyushins."

In fact, the Il-2 was built in greater numbers than any other combat aircraft during the Second World War, a total of 36,163 Il-2s of different versions being delivered. But the attrition rate for the Il-2 was higher than any other Soviet type. Statistics reveal that one Il-2 was lost for every thirty combat sorties. Early in the war, when Il-2 units lacked fighter protection, the loss rate was even higher. At this time, a Il-2 pilot was awarded with the "Hero of the Soviet Union" medal after ten successful missions.

Sergej Vladimirovich Ilyushin designed the Il-2 Stormovik. He was born on 31 March 1894, at Dilyalevo near Lake Kubensk. He began his aviation career in 1910 and during the First World War he joined the Imperial Russian Air Force as a mechanic. He received his pilots certificate in 1917.

During the bloody Russian civil war, Ilyushin was assigned to the 6th Salvage Group on the Northern Front, tasked with repairing damaged aircraft. In 1921, Ilyushin reported to the Institute of Red Air Fleet Engineers School in Moscow. Within two years, he had begun independent design work, designing three gliders, one of which, the AVF-21 Moskva, took part in a glider competition in Germany during 1925.

In 1933, he became the leader of a design group specializing in the development of a long range bomber and on 17 August 1936, Ilyushin created his own Design Bureau.

Most Red Air Fleet operations during the Civil War were low-level strafing and bombing missions. Contemporary Soviet military thinking emphasized the role of the aircraft in supporting ground troops. Battlefield reconnaissance, ground attack and close support were seen as the main functions of the Red Air Fleet.

A requirement for a dedicated ground attack aircraft was issued during 1928 and the First Section of the Scientific and Technological Committee of the Board of the Air Force, at that time headed by Ilyushin, worked up the tactical and technical requirements, but Ilyushin was not involved with the design. Three prototypes, the TSh-1, TSh-2 and TSh-3 were built. These aircraft were relatively good, but the weight of their armor caused a severe loss in overall performance, since they were basically under powered for their weight.

In early 1936, Stalin initiated the Ivanov project, a competition for a multi-purpose aircraft, which would be able to perform the assault, bombing, reconnaissance and escort roles. Five designs were submitted, the TsKB-27, the KhAI-5, the ANT-51, Ivanov-1 and the DG-58R, which was never completed because of the death of its designer. In the event, the Red Air Force chose the KhAI-5 and a total of 490 were built under the designation R-10.

Soviet air doctrine had, in sharp contrast to most European countries and the United States, rejected the idea that an independent air force could decide the outcome of a future war. As a result, Soviet designs were directed toward types that could assist the ground forces, including a class of dedicated ground attack aircraft.

On his own initiative, Ilyushin began to develop a so-called "Winged Tank." The outstanding feature of his design was an armored shell to protect the most vulnerable and vital parts of the aircraft; the crew, the engine, the fuel tanks and the oil system. This protective shell was to be an integral part of the airframe, not an addition to it.

On 27 January 1938, Ilyushin submitted his proposal to Stalin and assured him that a prototype would be ready for State Acceptance Trials in November. The proposal was accepted and Ilyushin was released from his other duties to be fully involved in the project. On 5 May 1938, an order was given for one prototype under the designation TsKB-55.

On 3 January 1939, the detailed project study for the TsKB-55 was submitted to the Commissariat of Defense Industry and on, 28 January 1939, a mock-up was finished. On 2 February 1939, the general lay-out of the mock-up was accepted by the Red Air Force and an order was given to the Ilyushin Design Bureau to build two prototypes.

The armored shell of the TsKB-55 prototype was fabricated from AB-1 (**Aviatsionnaya Bronya-1**), an armor plate with high proportions of nickel and molybdenum. The shell, called **Bronekorpus**, provided the "backbone" of the aircraft, with all other components being attached to it. It consisted of 4 to 5MM plates around the power plant, its coolant and oil radiators, the fuel and oil tanks, giving these components protection from below and the sides. The pilot and gunner were protected by 6MM to 8MM armor plates.

The wings, tail plane and what little of the forward fuselage that was not formed by the armored shell, were of duralumin construction, with the rear fuselage and vertical stabilizer being made of wood. All fixed surfaces had light alloy skinning and, apart from the pneumatically-operated metal skinned flaps, all moveable surfaces were fabric covered. The main undercarriage units had twin oleo-pneumatic shock-absorber legs and retracted rearward, laying semi recessed in fairings under the wing center section. K-4 armor glass was used in the canopy .

The heavily armored assault aircraft needed a powerful engine. An air-cooled power plant would be ideally suited for this type of aircraft, because it was less vulnerable to ground fire than a liquid-cooled engine, but, at the time, there was no air-cooled engine with sufficient power available. The only engine available in the Soviet Union with sufficient power was the

The first TsKB-55 prototype during factory flight tests at Khodinka airfield in late Autumn of 1939. At this time, the two seat assault aircraft did not carry national markings. The rear gunner was equipped with a single ShKAS 7.62MM gun. (Viktor Kulikov)

The rear gunner's position on the TsKB-57 prototype was occupied by a 41 gallon (155 liter) fuel tank which was separated from the cockpit by a 12MM armored bulkhead and covered by a large dorsal spine. (Viktor Kulikov)

AM-35, a 1,360 hp 12-cylinder, liquid-cooled, supercharged engine that drove a three-blade VISh-22T variable-pitch propeller. The prototype carried a total of 83.2 gallons (315 liters) of 95 octane fuel, distributed between tanks fore and aft of the pilot's cockpit and beneath the pilot's feet.

Initially, it was planned to design both the oil cooler and radiator to be retractable, so that the cooling system could be protected. During the development of the TsKB-55; however, this idea was dropped in favor of a more conventional layout.

Armament consisted of four 7.62MM ShKAS machine guns mounted in the outer wing panels and a similar weapon on a flexible mounting for the rear gunner. Four small, armored bomb bays were installed within the wing center section, each accommodating a single 220 pound (100 kg) bomb. These could be supplemented by two similar bombs on external wing racks or replaced by a pair of externally-mounted 551 pound (250 kg) bombs.

The first prototype made its maiden flight with Vladimir K. Kokkinaki at the controls on 2 October 1939. The second prototype flew for the first time on 30 December 1939, again with Vladimir K. Kokkinaki at the controls.

The factory test program revealed some problems, mainly in the cooling system. The oil cooler and radiator tended to overheat at full power during a steep climb. As a result, the radiator was enlarged, displacing the oil cooler, which was relocated under the fuselage protected by an armored box. Further problems with the AM-35 power plant were solved during the fac-

The TsKB-57 flew for the first time on 12 October 1940 with Vladimir K. Kokkinaki at the controls. The TsKB-57 was powered by an AM-38 engine which had better performance at low and medium altitudes than the earlier supercharged AM-35 engine. (Viktor Kulikov)

tory test program which ended on 26 March 1940.

Despite the fact that the handling characteristics were considered to be poor and the aircraft's longitudinal stability was particularly bad, the second prototype was handed over to the Scientific Research Institute of the Red Air Force at Zhukovsky for the State Acceptance trials. During this evaluation, which lasted twenty days, a total of thirty-eight flights were conducted.

These tests revealed that the most serious problem was a relatively low speed (225 mph, 362 km/h) at ground level. This was a direct result of the fact that the supercharged AM-35 power plant, developed for high altitude missions, gave its best performance at 14,763 feet (4,500 meters). At low altitudes, where the TsKB-55 would usually be flown, the supercharger absorbed a lot of power, giving the aircraft a low top speed. Other complaints included a short range, poor forward view, and weak offensive firepower.

But the Red Air Force had a good impression of the TsKB-55 as a battlefield bomber and ordered ten pre-series aircraft for operational evaluation under field conditions. The military designation, BSh-2 (*Bronirovaniy Stormovik 2*/Armored Assault Aircraft 2), was allocated to the TsKB-55.

The first prototype was modified to overcome the problems detected during the State Acceptance trials. This aircraft was equipped with one of the two recently finished AM-38 power plants which deleted the supercharger. Longitudinal stability was improved by enlarging the stabilizer by some 3.1 percent and by changing the center of gravity more to the front. This was done by installing the AM-38 engine 50MM further forward. Two of the ShVAK 7.62MM guns were replaced by two PTB-23 23MM cannons. The modification of the first prototype was nearly completed when a new order, issued by Kliment E. Voroshilov, Commissar and Chairman of the Red Air Force (who felt that the rear gunner not necessary,) came in to convert the TsKB-55 to a single seat configuration. As a result, the first TskB-55 was never flown before it was rebuilt to the single seat standard and the ten two seat BSh-2 were never delivered.

Instead of a pure assault aircraft, Stalin and Voroshilov preferred a single seat bomber, which could penetrate deeper into enemy territory at a higher altitude. Since there was no time to develop an entirely new aircraft, the Ilyushin decided to convert the first prototype, with the actual conversion taking less then a month. The rear gunner's position was now occupied by a 41 gallon (155 liter) fuel tank. The tank was separated from the cockpit by an 12MM armored bulkhead and covered by a large dorsal spine. The armament of four ShKAS 7.62 MM guns was retained. The single seat bomber received the designation TsKB-57 and flew for the first time on 12 October 1940. The factory test envelope lasted ten days and revealed that the TsKB-57 had greatly improved flight characteristics. The AM-38 supplied sufficient power at low and medium altitudes and, during testing, the TsKB-57 reached 262 mph (423 km/h) at ground level and 271.5 mph (437 km/h) at 9,186 feet (2,800 meters).

The preparations for production of the new type proceeded very slowly. In June of 1940, Ilyushin wrote a letter to the Central Committee of the All Union Communist Party and asked for permission to start production. But the Bureaucrats underestimated the importance of Ilyushin's design and did not even reply.

With the impressive results of the factory testing in hand, Ilyushin wrote to Stalin on 7 November 1940 and asked for immediate authorization to start production. After a December 1940 meeting at the Kremlin, production of the new type was finally authorized at GAZ 18 (GAZ, State Aircraft Factory) at Voronezh, even before the State Acceptance trials of the TsKB-57 were fully completed.

Development

TsKB-55

TsKB-57

Single Seat Il-2 Early

Single Seat Il-2 Late

Il-2M Late

Il-2M Type 3

Il-2 M-82/Il-4

Il-2 KR

Il-2 UT

Il-2 I

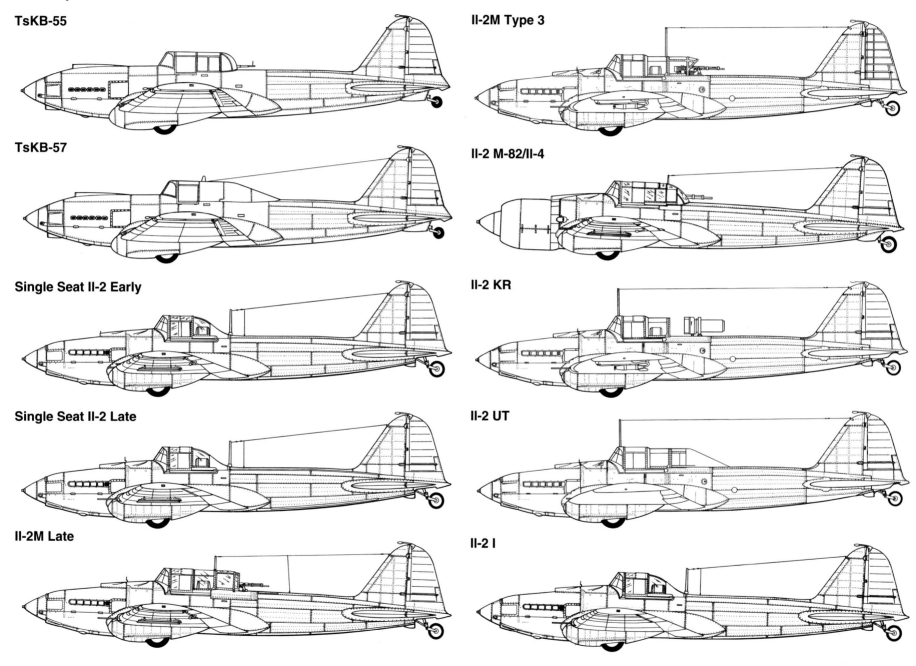

Single Seat Il-2s

TsKB-55P

During early 1941, the Soviet leadership realized that it was only a matter of time before Germany launched an attack against the Soviet Union. As a result, the Eighteenth Party Conference, held in February of 1941, was devoted almost entirely to defense matters. The budget allocation for defense, during the period 1928 to 1933, had been 5.4 percent of the gross national product, but in 1941, with the threat of war, it had risen to 43.4 percent. The defense industry began working at a furious pace and, by the time of Hitler's invasion, 2,839 new aircraft and 4,300 tanks had been built.

Immediately after the Commissariat of Aviation Industry gave the order, in December of 1940, to begin mass production of the new Ilyushin attack aircraft, the Ilyushin Design Bureau began to convert the second TsKB-55 prototype to serve as a pattern aircraft for the production type. All efforts of the Ilyushin Design Bureau were focused on the preparations for mass production of the new aircraft, which was going to be launched at GAZ 18 (GAZ *Gosudarstvenny Aviatsionny Zavod*/State Aircraft Factory) at Voronezh.

The conversion work took into account the results of both the factory and State Acceptance Trials, which had revealed a number of problems with the TsKB-57 prototype.

The AM-38 engine was installed 175MM lower and the canopy, including the pilot's seat was raised by 50MM in order to improve the pilot's forward view over the nose. The rear gunner's position was deleted and replaced with the same type of fuel tank that had been installed on the TsKB-57. Improved side armor was installed and the canopy was modified with armor glass replacing the standard glass.

This early production Il-2 was destroyed by German SD-2 fragmentation bombs during the opening days of Operation BARBAROSSA. Pre-war production Il-2s were equipped with a balance weight on the aileron and had the ShKAS 7.62MM machine gun in the outboard position. (ECPA/DAA 1093 L16)

Fuselage Development

TsKB-57

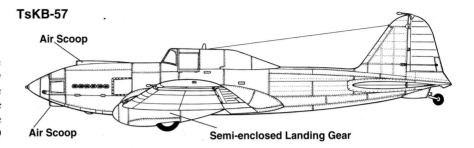

Air Scoop

Air Scoop   Semi-enclosed Landing Gear

Production Il-2

Repositioned Air Scoop   Higher Cockpit   Relocated Antenna Mast

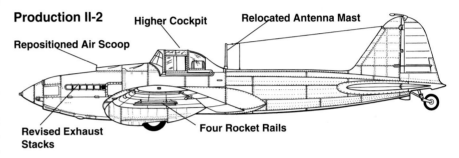

Revised Exhaust Stacks   Four Rocket Rails

Initially, it was planned to arm the TsKB-55P prototype with two PTB-23 23MM cannon and two ShKAS 7.62MM machine guns in the wings, but the PTB-23 weapon had proved to be very unreliable during testing and further investigation revealed that the heavy recoil of the PTB-23 could damage the wing structure. As a result, the ShVAK 20MM cannon was installed in the TsKB-55P. The prototype carried 420 20MM rounds and 500 7.62MM rounds for each weapon.

The ShKAS (**Shpitalny-Komaritski Aviatsionny Skorostreiny**/Shpitalny-Komaritski rapid fire machine gun) was developed in 1930 especially for the Soviet Air Force and had rate of fire of 1,800 rounds per minute. The weapon weighed 22 pounds (10 kg) and had muzzle velocity of 2,706 FPS (825 MPS). Large scale production of the ShKAS started in 1936.

The ShVAK (**Shpitalny-Vladimirova Aviatsionnsya Krupnokalibernaya**/Shpitalny-Vladimirov or Large Caliber Cannon) was based of the highly successful 7.62MM ShKAS. The 20MM cannon became available in 1936, weighed 92.5 pounds (42 kg) and had a rate of fire of 750 to 800 rounds per minute. It had a overall length of 5.7 feet (1,760MM) with a barrel length of 4 feet (1,245MM).

On 29 December 1940 Vladimir K. Kokkinaki took-off in the TsKB-55P for the first time and began the factory test program. The raised cockpit position considerably improved the forward view and a number of aerodynamic refinements gave the aircraft better flying qualities than the original TsKB-55. In January of 1941, the original military designation of BSh-2(**Bronirovaniy Stormovik 2**/Armored Assault Aircraft 2) was changed to Il-2. After a successful factory test program, the TsKB-55P was handed over to the Scientific Research Institute of the Red Air Force at Zhukovsky for State Acceptance Trials, which were flown by

This pre-war production Il-2 was captured by Hungarian troops at Skala-Kurilovcze on 5 August 1941 during their rapid advance into the Ukraine. All the armament, the landing light and pitot tube were removed. The spinner and propeller were painted Black. (Attila Bonhardt)

A. Dolgov. The TsKB-55P was tested fully armed, with cannon and machine guns installed in the wings along with a bomb load of 881 pounds (400 kg) in the wing bomb bays. During these tests it achieved speeds of 269 mph (433 km/h) at sea level and 280 mph (450 km/h) at 8070 feet (2,460 m). The intensive evaluation, which included at least two test flights per day, ended on 20 March 1941 and full production was authorized. With its successful conclusion, the Soviet Union became the first nation in the world with a genuine assault aircraft in its inventory.

Production Il-2

Even while the State Acceptance Trials were still under way, the first production Il-2s were being assembled at GAZ-18 at Voronezh. Ilyushin departed on 20 December 1940 for Voronezh to personally supervise the preparations for full production start-up. He was assisted by M.B. Shenkman, the factory director and N.D. Vostrov, the factory chief engineer.

On 10 March 1941, the first production Il-2 left the assembly lines and took off on its maiden flight with factory test pilot Lieutenant Colonel Konstantin K. Rykov at the controls. This flight was made just three months after the first production drawings and tools had been delivered to GAZ-18. A second Il-2 followed in the same month. During April, fourteen aircraft were produced, followed by seventy-four during May. A further 159 Il-2s were assembled during the first twenty days of June. Before the Germany launched Operation BARBAROSSA, a total of 249 Il-2s had been delivered to the Soviet Air Force.

The production Il-2 differed from the prototype in a number ways, the rear fuselage of the TsKB-57 was of wood, as was sections of the vertical fin. On production aircraft, these structures were of metal construction. The TsKB-57 had a more conical spinner, than the production Il-2.

While the TsKB-57 had a large air intake on top of the nose, the Il-2 had an air intake built into the fuselage which was further aft than on the TsKB-57. An external gun sight was mounted on top of the air intake on the prototype. This sight was replaced with PBP-1 (*Prizel dlya Bombometaniya S Pikirovaniya*/Bomb Sight for Dive Bombing) gun sight fitted in the cockpit. Some late Il-2 single seat versions were also equipped with the slightly modified PBP-1A gunsight. The PBP-1 could be pushed to the instrument panel during take off and landing and pulled out into its proper position when needed.

While the TsKB-57 had six small exhaust stubs, the Il-2 reconfigured the engine exhausts with five large exhaust stubs (first five) and one smaller stub (last stub). A square access panel behind the exhaust stubs on the TsKB-55 and TsKB-57 was replaced by a panel with a more triangular shape on production Il-2. The Il-2 was powered by a 1,600 hp AM-38 liquid cooled, 12 cylinder Vee power plant, which weighed 1,829 pounds (830 kg) and burned 95 octane fuel.

The windscreen was enlarged on the Il-2, with the three piece windscreen being made of 49MM armor glass. While the TsKB-57 prototype had a large dorsal spine, the production Il-2 featured a short glazed rear cockpit fairing to improve the rearward view for the pilot. A 65MM armor glass panel was installed immediately behind the pilot's seat for rear protection. While the two side canopy frames on the prototype opened upwards, production Il-2s had a single piece rear sliding canopy with 8MM armor side panels. The tail wheel and its housing were also slightly modified. The production Il-2 had an air filter installed in the starboard wing root. The landing light, mounted on the starboard wing of the TsKB-55 and TsKB-57 prototypes, was deleted on production Il-2s, with the port landing light being retained. The pitot tube was moved to a more outboard position and the aileron mass balance on both wing tips were increased in size. While the TsKB-55 and TsKB-57 prototypes carried a single position light on each wing tip, production aircraft had two position lights, one on the upper surface of the wing tip and another on the lower surface.

The prototype's armament, four ShKAS 7.62MM guns, was replaced by two ShVAK 20MM cannons with 500 rounds per gun and two ShKAS 7.62MM guns with 750 rounds per gun. The ShVAK proved to be rather unreliable in combat, many weapons, jamming with the first round rendering them useless for the rest of the mission.

This early Il-2 was equipped with a ShVAK 20MM cannon and has the 7.62MM machine gun in the inboard wing position. This configuration was rarely seen on ShVAK equipped aircraft. The ShVAK had a shorter barrel than the VYa-23 cannon. In addition, the aircraft has no aileron mass balance weights. The aircraft was armed with four RS-82 rockets. (Viktor Kulikov)

A Messerschmitt Bf 109 of JG 5 shot down this Il-2 over the Northern front. The main landing gear wheel was ripped off during the crash landing. This Il-2 carried an upper-surface camouflage of Black-Green and Medium Green over Light Blue undersurfaces. The national markings had a thin White outline. (Martin Villing)

Production Il-2s, produced at Voronezh for the attack role, mounted eight Type RO rocket rails under the wings for RS-82 unguided air-to-ground rockets (four under each wing). When the full armament of eight RS-82 missiles was carried, the aircraft's top speed was decreased by about 6 mph (11 km/h). The RS-82 was adopted in 1937. The projectile was twenty-two inches (560MM) long, with a 1.28 pound (0.585 kg) warhead and had a range of 3.23 miles (5,200 meters).

This early Il-2 fell into Rumanian army hands during the Winter of 1941/1942. It was fitted with four external reinforcing ribs on the fuselage (two low on the fuselage side and two high on the fuselage) as a field modification. These reinforcing ribs were necessary because the wooden rear fuselage could not withstand the stress of rough field operations and tended to break apart during hard landings. (Martin Kyburz)

External Reinforcing Ribs

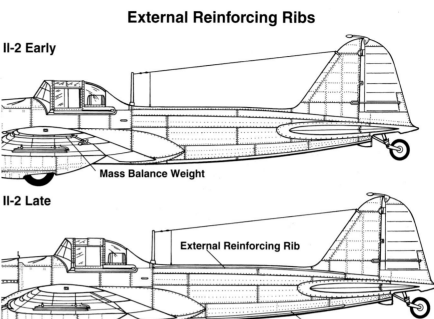

Il-2 Early

Mass Balance Weight

Il-2 Late

External Reinforcing Rib

Mass Balance Weight Deleted External Reinforcing Rib

Due to Government pressure to begin mass production of the Il-2, the workmanship of the first production aircraft was generally poor. This was also a result of insufficient training of the mainly unskilled workers used to build the Il-2. Compared with the TsKB-55P prototype, which served as a pattern for the standard production versions, the Il-2 had a higher empty weight and lower top speed, the latter was the result of the poor workmanship on the aircraft's skin, which was far rougher than the TsKB-55P prototype resulting in higher drag. A reduction of about 18.6 mph (30 km/h) in top speed on early production Il-2s was recorded by the Central Aero and Hydrodynamics Institute during a wind tunnel evaluation of a Voronezh built Il-2.

Il-2s produced before the war were camouflaged with Medium-Green uppersurfaces and Light Blue undersurfaces. There was a sharp line between the Green and the Blue camouflage on the fuselage and the wing. National markings were applied on the rear fuselage and the wing undersurfaces. The Red star had a thin Black outline and a single digit tactical number was applied on the fin. Most of the pre-war Il-2s had the spinner in Medium Green, but some spinners were Black. Shortly after the beginning of the Great Patriotic War, Il-2s were camouflaged in a two tone uppersurface camouflage of Medium Green and Black Green, with the undersurfaces in Light Blue. The demarcation between the upper and lower camouflage was soft edged. The Red star was applied on the wing undersurfaces, the rear fuselage and on the fin, and all had a thin White outline. The tactical number was applied to the rudder or sometimes on the fuselage, or even in both positions. The serial number was applied either in White or Black on the fin. Some Il-2s were repainted in the field and given Black fuselage undersurfaces, while the wings remained Light Blue. A few Il-2s received a three tone camouflage on the uppersurfaces of Medium Green, Black-Green and Earth Brown.

9

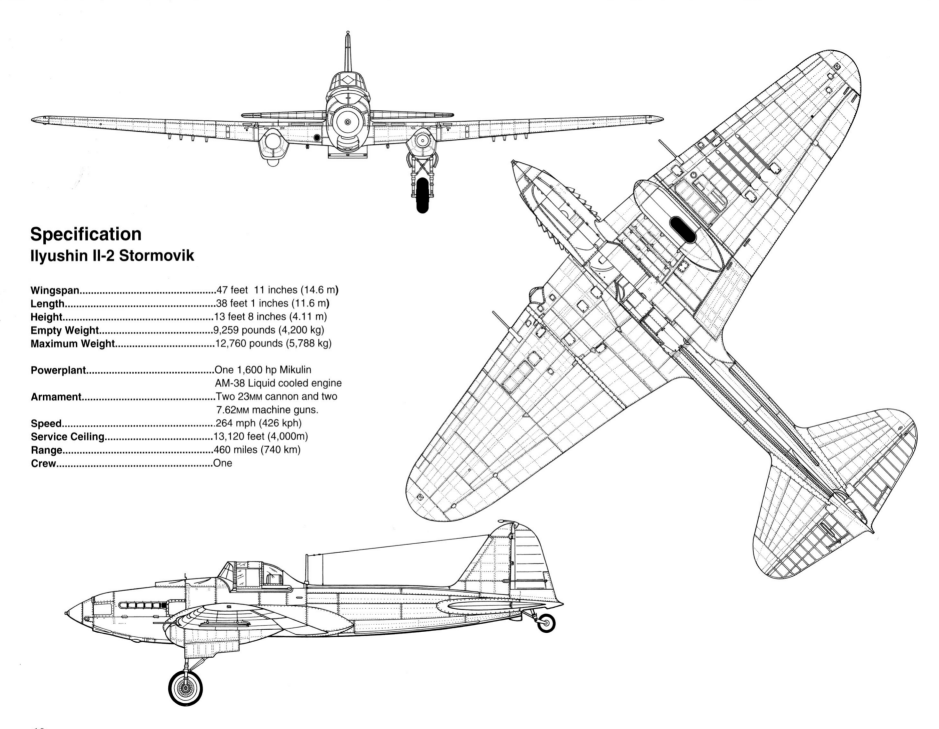

Specification
Ilyushin Il-2 Stormovik

Wingspan	47 feet 11 inches (14.6 m)
Length	38 feet 1 inches (11.6 m)
Height	13 feet 8 inches (4.11 m)
Empty Weight	9,259 pounds (4,200 kg)
Maximum Weight	12,760 pounds (5,788 kg)
Powerplant	One 1,600 hp Mikulin AM-38 Liquid cooled engine
Armament	Two 23mm cannon and two 7.62mm machine guns.
Speed	264 mph (426 kph)
Service Ceiling	13,120 feet (4,000m)
Range	460 miles (740 km)
Crew	One

This Il-2 was part of an exhibition of war booty held in Budapest, Hungary during May of 1942. The national markings had been cut off from the fuselage and the fabric covering was gone from the control surfaces. The glazed rear canopy section and lack of an armor on the canopy top were typical of early production Il-2s. (O. Horvath)

Shortly after the outbreak of the Great Patriotic War, a number of changes were introduced on the Il-2. The shortage of aluminum and steel forced State Aircraft Factory 18 to produce the rear fuselage and vertical fin and rudder in wood, which led to an increase in empty weight. This modification had a negative impact on Il-2s during front-line operations. The wooden rear fuselage could not withstand the stress of rough landings causing damage to the fuselage structure. This problem was overcome by installing four steel U-section reinforcing ribs on either side of the rear fuselage, two high on the fuselage and two low on the fuselage. This modification was first introduced by engineer A.K. Belenkov at a repair depot and later it was added to aircraft on the factory line. Initially the ribs were applied outside the fuselage but, later most Il-2s had the reinforcing ribs installed inside the fuselage. Pre-war Il-2s were fitted with a balance weight on the ailerons to improve control response, which were deleted shortly after the war began. In order to satisfy the needs of the front, the workers of GAZ-18 increased their shifts to ten or eleven hours a day.

The Il-2 received a considerable increase in fire power when the ShVAK 20MM cannon was replaced by the VYa-23 23MM cannon. This formidable weapon could penetrate one inch (25MM) of armor at a distance of 1,312 feet (400 meters). The weapon weighed 151 pounds (68.5 kg) and had a length of 7 feet (2,140MM). It had a muzzle velocity of 2,965 feet per second (905 meters per second) and a rate of fire of between 370 and 500 rounds per minute. While the ShVAK equipped Il-2 carried 500 rounds per gun, the 23MM equipped aircraft could only carry 300 rounds per gun due to the increased weight of the VYA-23 cannon and its ammunition.

With the adaptation of the VYa-23 cannon, the 7.62MM ShKAS gun was moved from the outboard wing position, between the ShVAK cannon and the pitot tube, to an inboard position near the VYa-23 cannon. This was necessary because the ammunition supply of the VYa-23 needed more space in the outer wing. There were also a number of Il-2s built having the

This early Il-2, serial 1076621, Yellow 3, had the fuselage undersurfaces and part of the flaps painted Black, while the rest of the undersurfaces remained Light Blue. The aircraft also has external aileron mass balance weights. (ECPA/DAA 1819 L31)

ShVAK cannon, but with the ShKAS gun fitted in the inboard position, a feature which was introduced when VYa-23 and ShVAK equipped aircraft were built alongside each other on the assembly line at GAZ-18.

Externally, the VYa-23 could be identified by its longer barrel and a fairing placed on the wing leading edge. Some ShVAK equipped Il-2 were also fitted with the fairing, but most lacked the fairing. The fairing in front of the tail wheel was also enlarged and slightly modified on Il-2s produced after the beginning of the Great Patriotic War.

Combat experienced, gained over the Eastern front, showed that there was insufficient rear protection for the pilot and a piece of armor plate was installed on the top of the rear sliding canopy. In addition, the side armor was increased and, as a result, the side windows were reduced in size. This modification was introduced in the early autumn of 1941 in an effort to reduce heavy operational losses of Il-2s.

The Il-2 had provisions for a RSI-4 radio transiver and, although the antenna mast and antenna wire were fitted on all Il-2s, the radio was rarely installed. Some Il-2s received a forward slanted antenna, but the most Il-2s had a vertical antenna mast. In many eases, only the formation leader's aircraft was fitted with a radio set. During the early part of the war, the absence of radios meant that the leader had to rely on signals to direct his wing men, while maintaining radio contact with the command post.

When "General Winter" approached on the Eastern front, a number of Il-2s were fitted with retractable skids, which replaced the main wheels. To lessen drag, a fairing was installed on the main wheel bay and the normal landing gear doors were deleted. The tail wheel was also replaced by a skid. This modification; however, enjoyed only limited success and adversely affected performance.

On 4 July 1941, the State Defense Committee had established a special Evacuation Council to supervise the relocation of critical industries to areas behind the Ural mountains - well beyond the range of German bombers. Before the move was completed in January of 1942, some 1,523 factories, of which 1,360 were defense industries, and ten million workers and their families would be uprooted and transported more than 1,000 miles to the East. Because much of the aircraft industry was concentrated around Moscow, its evacuation did not get fully under way until Autumn of 1941, when the Soviet capital was clearly menaced.

Voronezh was within range of the Luftwaffe bombers and on 19 September 1941, Heinkel He-111s bombed State Aircraft Factory 18 for the first time. On 19 October 1941, an order was given to evacuate GAZ-18 to Kuibyshev and the project to dismantle the factory started on 26 October 1941. The Mikulin engine factories in Moscow, GAZ-24 and GAZ-207, which produced armored parts of the fuselage, were also moved east of the Ural mountains. Difficulties with the evacuation and restarting production were so serious that, for thirty-five days, no new Il-2s could be produced.

At Kuibyshev on the Volga river, all was chaos. The preparations to resume production began in a roofless assembly complex seven kilometers north of Kuibyshev, which had been originally intended to be a power station. The workers often lived beside their machines in crude wooden huts, subsisting on bread and a thin soup made from beet greens. There were monumental shortages of tools and materials and craftsmanship and fine tolerances were forgotten in the rush to produce as many Il-2s as possible. As a result, the performance and flying characteristics of the Il-2s produced at Kuibyshev were inferior to those assembled at Voronezh before the evacuation. But not even bitter cold temperatures, up to forty below zero, and snow could stop the Soviets from turning out Il-2s in that roofless building.

A dramatic wartime telegram sent by Stalin to the plant on 22 December 1941, reflected the

A Il-2 returns from a mission during the harsh Winter of early 1942. Shortly after the outbreak of the Great Patriotic War, Il-2s were repainted in Black-Green and Medium Green uppersurface camouflage with the national markings being carried on the lower wing and fuselage. The Red stars had a thin White outline. (G.F. Petrov)

Canopy Development

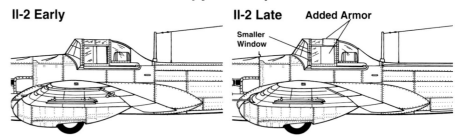

Il-2 Early

Il-2 Late   Added Armor

Smaller Window

great importance of this aircraft in the dictator's point of view, "The Red Army needs the Il-2 as it needs air and bread. I urge you to produce more Ilyushins!" A decree issued by the Supreme Soviet on 25 December 1941, declared all workers as mobilized to war and the workers were organized into two twelve hour shifts.

The first Il-2 left the Kuibyshev plant on 10 December 1941. This aircraft was assembled from components actually built at Voronezh and made its acceptance flight the same day, with factory test pilot Yevgeni Lomakin at the controls.

During the last month of 1941, only twenty-nine Il-2s were produced at GAZ-18. During the first year of war a total of 1,134 Il-2s were built, 885 of them since the German attack to the Soviet Union.

The difficulties in assembling the Il-2s continued during the first days of the new year. As of 5 January 1942, the Kuibyshev plant was capable of delivering five Il-2s a day, this figure increasing to six aircraft on 19 January and starting on 26 January, the production rate rose to seven aircraft a day. By the Spring of 1942, the daily output of Il-2s stood at forty aircraft a day.

A number of changes were introduced on the Il-2s manufactured at Kuibyshev during the course of their production run. The rear portion of the glazed center canopy was replaced, during early 1942, by a solid armor fairing in order to protect the pilot from fighter attacks from the rear. During early 1942, the RS-132 unguided rocket became available in numbers. The RS-132 had a length of 2.83 feet (864 мм) and had a five pound (2.25 kg) warhead, giv-

This early Il-2, White 7, of the 174 ShAP (Assault Aviation Regiment) prepares for a mission on the Leningrad front during the Winter of 1941-1942. The aircraft has a non-standard oblique antenna mast, rarely seen on Il-2s. (G. F. Petrov)

ing the rocket a lethal diameter of 656 feet (200 meters). The RS-132 could be carried on the RO rocket rails used with the earlier RS-82 rocket. A direct hit by either a RS-82 or RS-132 could knock out light and medium tanks. But, because the rockets scattered in flight, they were used to attack tight columns and armor/troop concentrations.

Late production Il-2s had the PBP-1 or PBP-lA gun sight replaced by a very rudimentary VV-1 gun sight. The VV-1 sight was introduced on single seat Il-2s for the first time in August of 1942, just a few weeks before the production switched to the two seat Il-2M. The PBP-1 gun sight had proven to be very unpopular with service pilots because it had a tendency to cause serious head injuries in the event of a crash landing. As a result, it was replaced with the VV-1 aiming device which consisted of three aiming circles drawn on the diamond shaped area of the armor glass windshield. The external front sight for the PBP-1 gun sight was retained and repositioned further to the rear. The VV-1 gun sight became the standard gun sight on two seat Il-2Ms and all later two seat versions.

These late production Il-2s carried the four horizontal reinforcing ribs inside the fuselage and some of the very late production single seat Il-2s relocated the air filter to the starboard side wing root. This sand filter was fitted to all Il-2 two seat variants on the production line, but it was rarely seen on single seat Il-2s. The sand filter became a vital modification when it became clear that the sand and dust on the unprepared airfields destroyed the AM-38 power plants. During the hot and dry Summer of 1942, when the engines were faced with a particularly high amounts of dust, no less then 250 engine failures were reported by front-line Assault Aviation Regiments.

Production of single seat Il-2s continued until the late Summer 1942, when the Il-2M replaced the single seaters on the assembly lines.

Il-2s, fresh off the assembly line, receive final checks at State Aircraft Factory 18 at Kuibyshev. The landing light on production Il-2s was mounted on the starboard wing only. (G.F. Petrov)

These Il-2s are on the assembly line at the vast assembly buildings of State Aircraft Factory 18. These Il-2s were painted in the factory with a Black-Green and Medium Green uppresurface camouflage. No national markings were carried on the wing uppersurface. The Red Star was carried on the fuselage, fin/rudder and wing undersurfaces. These were painted at the factory with a thin White outline. (G. F. Petrov)

The VYa-23 23MM cannon had a longer barrel than the earlier 20MM weapon carried on the Il-2. The small barrel, inboard of the cannon, is the ShKAS 7.62MM machine gun. This aircraft is armed with four RS-82 unguided rockets which became standard armament on single seat Il-2 variants. The early ShVAK 20MM cannon equipped Il-2s had the 7.62MM ShKAS mounted outboard on the wing between the cannon and the pitot tube. The Il-2 carried 300 rounds for the VYa-23 and 750 rounds for the ShKAS. The serial number, 1863722, was painted on the landing gear housing. (Manfred Griehl)

Il-2 Two Seat Conversions

The most serious problem with the Il-2 was its lack of the rear protection. German fighter pilots quickly learned that the aircraft could be easily downed by an attack from the rear and this quickly became the standard tactic for attacking Il-2s. The May 1940 decision to remove the rear gun position from the TsKB-55 in favor of additional fuel and range, led to serious losses, but proved that Ilyushin's original two seat configuration was the best configuration for an assault aircraft. Endless complaints about the alarming attrition rate were sent from front-line regiments to the Ilyushin Design Bureau. In their battle reports, Il-2 pilots bitterly complained about the complete lack of rear defense.

Some regiments; however, did not wait for an answer from the Design Bureau and added a rear gun position as a field modification. In the 198th Assault Aviation Regiment, the Regimental engineering officer calculated that the change in the center of gravity was acceptable. He then cut a semi-circular hole in the rear of the canopy and improvised a gunner's position, armed with a 7.62MM machine gun. The rear gunner sat on the ammunition box and holes were also cut in the improvised seat for the aircraft's control rods.

Other Regiments, such as the 57th Assault Aviation Regiment, cut off the rear portion of the canopy and a part of the fuselage in order to make room for the rear gunner, a 7.62MM machine gun and ammunition. The ShKAS 7.62MM weapon was chosen because it was available in large numbers. Often the turret ring was a modified unit taken from a Polikarpov R-5 biplane.

The 17th Air Army, under the command of Lieutenant General S.A. Krasovskiy was assigned to the Southwestern front, and was comprised of the 208th and 637th Assault Air Divisions. The units converted sixty-six Il-2s into the two-seat configuration during the Autumn of 1942. The 17th Air Army saw heavy combat on the Stalingrad front, supporting the Soviet counteroffensive to encircle the German 6th Army under the command of General Friedrich Paulus.

The 243rd Assault Aviation Division introduced their rear gun Il-2s into combat as soon as the unit became active in the Northwestern front in June of 1942. Colonel J. Davidov of the 243rd Assault Air Division, together with his engineering officer, V. Koblikov, demonstrated,

one of the aircraft to the board of Air Force Commanders and a number of aviation designers in September of 1942. They detailed how a single seat aircraft could be converted at a Aviation Division level field repair depot. This procedure was subsequently recommended to all units which were operating the single seat Il-2s

The conversion of single seat Il-2s to the two seat standard continued in the various Air Army depots even after the first rear gun equipped Il-2Ms were delivered directly from the factory to the front in the Autumn of 1942.

Field Modified Gun Position

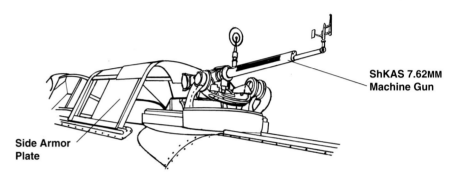

ShKAS 7.62MM Machine Gun

Side Armor Plate

This single seat Il-2 of the 57th ShAP (Assault Aviation Regiment) was fitted with a rear gunner's position. Within front-line Assault Regiments such conversions were locally made as a field modification. The rear portion of the canopy and a portion of the rear fuselage was cut away to make room for the gun and gunner. Often the gun and turret ring were taken from Polikarpov R-5 biplanes. (Hannu Valtonen)

This Il-2 of the 57th ShAP (Assault Aviation Regiment) was modified with a rear gun position. The flexible ShKAS 7.62MM gun was fed with ammunition belts from boxes which also served as a seat for the rear gunner. (G.F. Petrov)

Combat

The first Il-2s were allocated to the 4th Assault Aviation Regiment in May of 1941. Instructor pilots and ground crews were sent to State Aircraft Factory 18 at Voronezh, where they were given conversion training on the new type. Training proved to be difficult since the pilots were only familiar with bi-planes and the sluggish flight characteristics and the lack of precise and rapid control response caused serious problems. During take off the aircraft had a serious yaw to the right because of torque, which added more problems for the inexperienced pilots. When the instructor pilots completed their conversion training they were sent to Bogoduchov with the first batch of Il-2s in order to start training the remaining pilots and ground crews of the 4th Assault Aviation Regiment. This unit was the first Regiment within the Red Air Force which became fully operational with the Il-2 and had a total of sixty-five aircraft on strength in mid-June of 1941, just a few days before the Germans launched their attack. By that time the pilots were barely able to handle their aircraft and had not developed any combat tactics with their new mounts.

Originally, the 4th Assault Aviation Regiment was to have been a training unit to help other units convert to the Il-2. But when the invasion of the Soviet Union started on 22 June 1941, the Regiment, under the command of Major S.G. Getman, received orders to move from Bogoduchov to the front on 1 July 1941 and immediately started to attack enemy armor and troop concentrations in the Berezin River and Bobruysk areas.

None of the pilots had ever trained in combat tactics or weapons delivery and most had not even fired their guns in training. Initially, it had been planned that factory test pilots at Voronezh would also train the 4th Assault Aviation Regiment pilots in tactics and weapons use, but this never took place before the pilots had to return to their units. As a result, the pilots had to learn the best combat tactics and the right angle to attack enemy armor and troop concentration while flying actual combat missions.

Losses in aircraft and crews were heavy. Within a three day period, the 4th Assault Aviation Regiment lost twenty pilots. By 10 July, only twenty-one of the original sixty-five

The White inscription on the fuselage of this Il-2 reads, *Valerij Chkalov*, a famous Soviet test pilot who was killed testing the Polikarpov I-180 fighter on 15 December 1938. The aircraft carries a small tactical number, White 82, along with a White identification stripe on the rudder. (G. F. Petrov)

Il-2s allocated to the Regiment were serviceable. By early September of 1941, only a few Il-2s had survived the slaughter. The remaining Il-2s were allocated to the 215th Assault Aviation Regiment and the pilots of the 4th Assault Aviation Regiment flew to Voronezh to

This captured Il-2 carried full Luftwaffe markings as well the Yellow fuselage identification band, applied on all Axis aircraft assigned to the Eastern front. The underwing rocket rails have been removed from this aircraft. (Hannu Valtonen)

Stormovik pilots hold a briefing in front of N.A. Zub's White camouflaged Il-2. N.A. Zub later became a Hero of the Soviet Union. The Black inscription on the fuselage reads *Smjert Fashistskim Okkypantam!* (Death to the Facist Occupiers!). (Yefim Gordon)

A Stormovik pilot receives his orders prior to a mission. This Il-2 had been modified with the external reinforcing ribs on the fuselage. The White inscription on the fuselage reads, *Za Otradnov* (For Otradnov, a pilot in the Regiment who was killed in action). There are aiming lines on the side window of the windshield. (Zdenek Hurt)

This Il-2, Red 8, of the 174th ShAP has a modified rear canopy section that has been fitted with extra armor. In addition, an armor plate was fitted to the top of the canopy frame. These features were introduced to enhance the survivability of the Il-2, since it had become clear that the single seat Il-2 was extremely vulnerable to fighter attacks from the rear. (G.F. Petrov)

collect new aircraft. With only twenty-four new Il-2s on strength, the unit returned to the front on 17 September 1941. Due to its outstanding performance during the early stages of the Great Patriotic War, the 4th Assault Aviation Regiment was redesignated the 7th Guards Assault Aviation Regiment on 7 March 1942.

In the late Summer of 1941 the following units were committed to combat: the 61st, 65th, 74th, 215th, 243th and 502nd Assault Aviation Regiments. The 61st Assault Aviation Regiment received their baptism of fire on 13 July 1941 in the Smolensk area. A flight of the 74th Assault Aviation Regiment, led by Lieutenant G. M. Moshinez, was able to destroy fifteen enemy tanks and vehicles advancing toward Moscow on 5 October. During October, the 74th Assault Aviation Regiment flew some 700 missions, destroying fifty-five tanks, twenty half-tracks and a number of vehicles, for the loss of only nineteen Il-2s.

At the beginning of the war, an Assault Aviation Regiment consisted of two squadrons with nine Il-2s on strength with an additional two Il-2s allocated to the Regiment's command flight. In reality, due to poor maintenance and a lack of spare parts, no more than ten to fifteen Il-2s per regiment were operational at any given time during the early stages of the war.

As soon the State Aircraft Factory began delivering a steady flow of aircraft during the Spring of 1942, the Assault Aviation Regiments were expanded to three squadrons of ten aircraft along with two for the Regiment's command.

The Il-2 was one of the most unpleasant surprises the German Wehrmacht had to face during its advance into the Soviet Union. In fact, the Il-2 was the only effective weapon in the inventory of the Red Air Force which could deal with armor. The Il-2 had escaped German intelligence until the type appeared for the first time over the battlefield. The tight security measures of the Stalin administration in defense matters and a certain disinterest in new Soviet aircraft developments in the German intelligence services were generally responsible for this

surprise. In addition, the German Air Attaché in Moscow, Colonel Heinrich Aschenbrenner, was briefed to stop intelligence activities in the Soviet Union after the signing of the Hitler-Stalin Pact on 23 August 1938, in order not to disturb the well developed political climate between these two countries. The German Air Force 5th Division intelligence service general-

A winter camouflaged Il-2,White 6, heads for an enemy position on the Stalingrad front in January of 1943. Part of the national marking on the rudder was overpainted with Whitewash. (G. F. Petrov)

A Il-2 is refueled in the open during the harsh Winter conditions on the East Front The spinner on this Stormovik is painted Red. No RS-82 rockets are mounted on the Type RO underwing rocket rails.

ly underestimated the strength of front-line Red Air Force regiments by nearly fifty percent. The German estimates for the aircraft production of the Soviet Union in 1941 was two thirds lower than the actual production figures for that year.

The Il-2 gained German respect for the sheer stubbornness of their pilots, who pressed home their attacks through lethal anti-aircraft fire. The Il-2 attacks were damaging, although their

This Soviet pilot surrendered to Hungarian troops after coming down in the southern sector near Kharkov in the Summer of 1941. His Il-2 had the external reinforcing ribs on the rear fuselage first introduced as a field modification. The Red star on the fuselage had a thin Black outline. (George Punka)

A pair of late production Il-2s were evaluated by the Luftwaffe. Both have a three stack exhaust system, a configuration rarely seen on Il-2s. Most Stormoviks had a four stack exhaust system. (Heinz J. Nowarra)

ShKAS guns were only effective against soft skinned vehicles, but the later VYa-23 cannon could cause considerable damage to armored vehicles, as could the RS-82 and RS-132 rockets. The armor on the Il-2 enabled it to withstand numerous hits from light guns and even 20MM cannon shells hitting at oblique angles.

The Il-2 units used a "serpentine" or "circle" formation to attack tank columns on the march, a "circle" or "figure 8" formation against concentrations of equipment forming-up or refueling. A "circle" formation was employed against tank formations which were advancing or dispersed over the terrain.

The circle was the main tactical formation for Il-2s. In addition to the "closed circle," a so-called "free circle" was also employed, where the aircraft maintained only the same general direction of flight and the pilots were granted complete freedom of action. The pilots attacked the tanks by making three or four individual attacks in a circle, increasing bombing and strafing accuracy. The continuous maneuvering in the process of flight made it difficult for anti-aircraft artillery to track the Il-2s and ensured the rapid suppression of the detected air defense weapons. In addition, the "free circle" could be quickly reformed into a "closed" circle to repel attacks by enemy fighters without stopping the attacks on the ground targets.

The Il-2 also proved to be very effective in attacks of German trains and the Wehrmacht railway network in the occupied areas of the Soviet Union. Il-2s were also used to attack marshaling yards with success.

The Il-2 was far from being a sitting duck for fighters, but most hastily trained Il-2 pilots were not trained to use the extraordinary maneuverability of the Il-2. Experienced pilots could perform aerobatic maneuvers and, in combat, they successfully engaged enemy fighters in air-to-air combat. On one such an occasion, Sergeant N. Ryaboshapko of the 299th Assault Aviation Regiment was credited with the shooting down of four Messerschmitt Bf 109s during a mission in March of 1942. For this action, Ryaboshapko became a "Hero of the Soviet Union."

In the early stages of the Great Patriotic War, the Il-2 pilots had to perform most of their missions without fighter escort. Only a few fighters were available for escort missions during this critical period. For instance, in September of 1942, obsolete I-16s of the 728th Fighter Aviation Regiment were used to escort Il-2 formations in the Stalingrad area.

German airfields also became a popular target for the Il-2s. In August of 1942, Il-2s of the

Luftwaffe personnel examine a late production Il-2 fitted with a VV-1 gun sight and four reinforcing ribs on the rear fuselage. The aircraft has had its armament stripped from the wings and has had the cowling panels removed so that Luftwaffe personnel can study the engine. (Manfred Griehl)

A line-up of three late production single seat Il-2s. Some late production single seat Il-2s were fitted with a sand filter mounted on the starboard wing root. This filter was not fitted to most single seaters, but became standard on all two seat Stormoviks. Late production Il-2s also had the aileron mass balance weight deleted. (G.F. Petrov)

The Il-2 captured by Hungarian troops was repainted in Royal Hungarian Air Force markings. The fin was only partially marked having a single White band rather than the Red-White-Green bands normally carried on Hungarian aircraft. (George Punka)

228th Assault Aviation Division attacked several airfields on the southwestern front and destroyed not less than sixty German aircraft on the ground.

Il-2 losses were very heavy and the attrition rate continued to climb as more Assault Aviation Regiments were hastily formed. Many Il-2 pilots lacked sufficient flight training on the type when they were assigned to a Regiment and entered combat. It was most common to train these pilots for ten hours on the Lisunov Li-2 transport plane before they were sent into combat in the Il-2. Most of these pilots were only familiar with the most simplified tactics and attacked their targets in a shallow dive, which made the aircraft a steady target for concentrated ground fire. During this stage of the Great Patriotic War, a Il-2 pilot was awarded the "Hero of the Soviet Union" medal after ten successful missions, but very few pilots achieved this goal. In the second half of the war, 100 combat missions had to be flown to earn the award.

This Il-2 crash landed in friendly territory on the Eastern Front during 1942. It was unusual in that it carried a three tone uppersurface camouflage of Medium Green, Black-Green and Earth Brown. Three tone camouflage schemes were rarely used on single seat Il-2s. (Zdenek Hurt)

Il-2I Fighter

The Il-2I (I = *Istrebitel* or Fighter) was developed by the Ilyushin Design Bureau after assault Il-2s scored several shoot downs of slow flying Luftwaffe transports and bombers, such as Heinkel He-111s or Junkers Ju-52s, used on the Eastern front to fly supply missions for the various German pockets, which were surrounded by the advancing Red Army. With its deviating firepower of two 23MM cannon and two 7.62MM machine guns, German transports were an easy prey for Il-2s.

Il-2s of the 288th Assault Aviation Regiment engaged and shot down a number of German Junkers Ju-52s during the Winter of 1942 when the Luftwaffe started to supply the encircled 100,000 soldiers of 2nd Army Corps who were trapped by the Soviet winter offensive in the Demyansk pocket.

In May of 1943, the Ilyushin Design Bureau submitted a proposal to the Red Air Force for a single seat fighter based on the Il-2, but with an uprated AM-38F engine. Armed with two VYa-23 cannons, the fighter version of the Stormovik had more fire power than fighters currently in use with the Red Air Force. It was planned to operate the fighter variant in low and medium altitudes against transports, Stukas and bombers, such as the He-111.

As soon as the proposal was accepted by State authorities, the Ilyushin Design Bureau begun to convert a single seat Il-2 to the fighter configuration. The two ShKAS 7.62MM guns were removed, as well the eight type RO underwing rocket rails. The aileron mass balance weights were also deleted. The aircraft retained its capability to carry two external underwing bomb racks, each stressed to carry up to 1,102 pounds (500 kg). Gun armament consisted of a pair of VYa-23 cannons with an ammunition supply of 150 rounds per gun. A VV-1 gun sight was mounted on the air intake scoop.

To handle increased stress, the wooden wing was reinforced. The aircraft was powered by a 1,700 hp AM-38F engine. The Il-2I weighed 11,867 pounds (5,383 kg), which was 882

The Il-2I fighter had the two ShKAS 7.62MM machine guns deleted along with the underwing rocket rails. Its armament consisted of a pair of VYa-23 23MM cannons with 150 rounds per gun. The aircraft was powered by an improved 1,700 hp AM-38F engine. (Viktor Kulikov)

pounds (400 kg) lighter than the standard assault version. This weight reduction was accomplished by the removing of a considerable portion of the armor protection which was unnecessary for fighter missions.

The Il-2I started factory tests in July of 1943. The fighter reached 258 mph (415 km/h) at 1,265 feet (4,300 meters). Up to altitudes of 13,123 feet (4,000 meters), the top speed was superior to the Heinkel-111 or Junkers Ju-87. Although the tests proved to be successful, the fighter project did not develop beyond the factory testing stage because the Red Air Force now had sufficient fighters with better performance strength and the Assault Aviation Regiments had a growing demand for the two seat Il-2s. As a result the project was canceled.

Fuselage Development

Il-2 Early

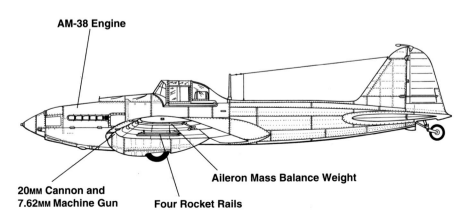

AM-38 Engine

20MM Cannon and
7.62MM Machine Gun

Four Rocket Rails

Aileron Mass Balance Weight

Il-2I Fighter

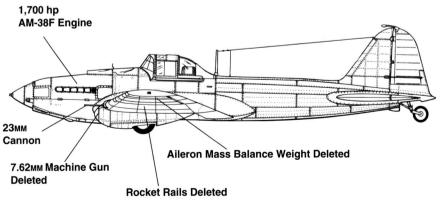

1,700 hp
AM-38F Engine

23MM
Cannon

7.62MM Machine Gun
Deleted

Aileron Mass Balance Weight Deleted

Rocket Rails Deleted

Il-2M-82/Il-4

The German invasion of the Soviet Union advanced through Smolensk to the Western edge of Moscow, laid siege to Leningrad, and captured Kiev and much of the Ukraine. The fall of Smolensk to the Germans on 16 July 1941 placed Moscow in imminent danger.

At 0530 on 30 September 1941 the Germans launched *Unternehmen Taifun* (Operation TYPHOON), when *Generalfeldmarschall* Fedor von Book's Army Group Center planned a double envelopment of Soviet troops guarding the approaches of Moscow.

With the impending attack, the evacuation of Moscow's factories, producing vital war goods, became critical. With the movement of the Mikulin engine work (GAZ-24) from Moscow to a location behind the Ural mountains, a shortage of AM-38 power plants was expected.

As a result, the Ilyushin Design Bureau started a project to adapt alternative engines to the Il-2. When the Wehrmacht penetrated towards Moscow, a high priority was assigned to the project.

A pre-war standard production single seat Il-2 served as an engine test bed. One of the power plants chosen for installation was the M-82 fourteen cylinder two row radial engine which was, at that time the only reliable engine which could serve as a substitute for the AM-38 if a shortage of engines occurred.

The testbed was designated the Il-2M-82, which was subsequently changed into Il-4. The 1,676 hp M-82 engine was developed by Arcadiy D. Shvetsov and his team in their Design Bureau at Perm in central Russia. Shortly after the end of the State Acceptance Trials, large scale production of the M-82 power plant was started in May of 1941. Due to the fact that Perm was in Siberia, it was far beyond the range of German bombers and therefore there was

The Il-4 was powered by a Shvetsov 1,676 hp M-82 air-cooled radial engine. It was converted from a pre-war production Il-2 single seater and retained the aileron mass balance weights. The national markings on the rear fuselage had a thin small Black outline. (Viktor Kulikov)

Fuselage Development

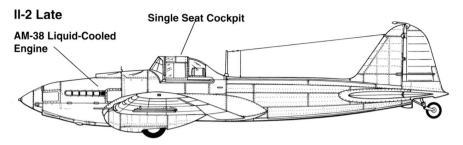

Il-2 Late
AM-38 Liquid-Cooled Engine — Single Seat Cockpit

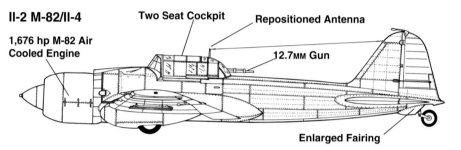

Il-2 M-82/Il-4
1,676 hp M-82 Air Cooled Engine — Two Seat Cockpit — Repositioned Antenna — 12.7MM Gun — Enlarged Fairing

no danger of shortages.

To match the Il-2 airframe with the bulky M-82 radial engine was not an easy task. It was necessary to separate the armored cantilever engine shell from the firewall immediately ahead of the wing leading edge. The M-82 engine mounting was unarmored and was fitted with a NACA type cowling with airflow regulating flaps at the trailing edge. In order to retain the aircraft's thrust line, the engine was mounted lower, giving the Il-2M-82 a humped nosed appearance.

The spinner was more conical and the VISh-22T propeller was replaced by an AV-5-160 propeller. A large air intake duct was installed in the top of the engine cowling and there was a single exhaust stack mounted on each side of the cowling just below the cowl flaps. On the starboard side, the AM-38 wing root air intake was faired over.

Offensive armament remained the same as on the early production Il-2, two 20MM ShVAK cannon and a two ShKAS 7.62MM guns in the wings and the underwing rocket rails; however, the external front sight for the PBP-lB gun sight was deleted.

The lighter engine and the removal of the engine cooling system, together with the simpler construction, led to a weight reduction of 882 pounds (400 kg). The two seat Il-4 had a weight of 12,908 pounds (5,855 kg), some 293 pounds (133 kg) less than the AM-38 powered single seat Il-2.

The rear gunner's station was reinstated although the position was somewhat further back and fitted with protective armor for the rear gunner. In addition, the two side windows of the front canopy were slightly enlarged when compared with the production single seat Il-2. The Berezin UBT (UB = *Universalnij Berezina* while the T stands for a turret version) 12.7MM machine gun was surrounded by a glazed covering and, as a result, the angle of fire was limited to 38 degrees upward and to 22 degrees to either side. An ammunition supply of 280 rounds was provided. The UBT entered the Red Air Force inventory during 1940. It weighed 56 pounds (25.5 kg), had a length of 4.46 feet (1,365MM), had a rate of fire of 800 rpm and a muzzle velocity of 2,821 feet per second (860 meters per second). This highly successful weapon was used on the Pe-2, Tu-2 and Pe-8 bombers.

The reintroduction of a rear gunner made it necessary to relocate the fuel tank to a position under the pilot. The fuel capacity was also increased to 191 gallons (724 liters). The antenna mast moved from the fuselage to the top of the enlarged canopy frame.

The Il-4 prototype was painted in Medium Green on the uppersurfaces over Light Blue undersurfaces. The national markings were carried on the rear fuselage and the wing undersurfaces with a thin Black outline. No tactical or special markings were carried on the Il-4.

The Il-4 flew for the first time on 8 September 1941, with Vladimir K. Kokkinaki at the controls. During factory testing, the Il-4 reached a speed of 237 mph (382 km/h) at ground level and 261 mph (421 km/h) at 8,530 feet (2,600 meters). The test program also revealed some center of gravity problems and poor longitudinal stability. The lighter engine, reduced armor and rear gun position had resulted in a rearward shift of the center of gravity. Even with these problems the tests went forward and were completed in eight days.

Due to the evacuation of the Ilyushin Design Bureau and the chaos that occurred when the German army neared Moscow, the State Acceptance Trials were seriously delayed and did not start before late February of 1942.

The performance of the Il-4 was rated as slightly inferior to that of the Il-2, but the Il-4 was authorized by the Commissariat of Aviation Industry for production after the successful State Acceptance Trials, which ended in April of 1942. When it became clear that there would be no significant shortage of AM-38 engines; however, it was decided not to produce the Il-4 and as a result the Il-4 prototype remained the only example built.

When it became clear that the radial engine Stormovik project had been canceled, the designation Il-4 was allocated to the twin engined long range Ilyushin DB-3F bomber, which was used by the Long Range Bomber Regiments. The M-82 engine became a success of its own, with over 70,000 engines being built. They were used to power the Lavochkin La-5 and La-7, as well the Tupolev Tu-2 bomber.

The Shvetsov M-82 radial powered variant of the Il-2 was known as the Il-2M-82 (Il-4). It later served as a pattern aircraft for the two seat Il-2. The rear gunner was armed with a Berezin UBT 12.7MM machine gun. The radio antenna mast was moved from the fuselage to the top of the rear canopy frame. (Viktor Kulikov)

The M-82 air-cooled radial engine of the Il-4 was unarmored. The two row fourteen cylinder engine developed 1,676 hp and was housed in a tight fitting NACA cowling with cowl flaps around the trailing edge. This same engine was used to power the La-5 and La-7 fighters (G.F. Petrov)

The Il-2M-82/Il-4 prototype is up on jacks for drop tests of its main landing gear on 16 September 1941. The M-82 engine drove a three blade AV-5-160 propeller. The starboard wing root air intake was deleted on the Il-4. (Viktor Kulikov)

Il-2M

The most serious shortcoming of the single seat Il-2 was its total lack rear defense. Luftwaffe pilots quickly discovered this weakness and developed tactics to attack the Il-2 in its most vulnerable position - the high rear quarter. Without fighter escort, the attrition rate in Assault Aviation Regiments was very high.

Pilots bitterly complained to the Ilyushin Design Bureau about this tactical weakness and the disadvantage it put them in. It was ironic that Ilyushin had designed the original Il-2 with a rear gunner position. The dramatic combat losses suffered by the Assault Aviation Regiments and the declining combat effectiveness of the Il-2 prompted a special conference at the Kremlin in early 1942 to consider measures to alleviate attrition and improve the combat capability of the Il-2. Both temporary measures and long term solutions were discussed

The conference was attended by led Stalin, the Commissar of Aviation Industry Alexei Shachurin and his deputy Aleksandr Yakovlev, as well as a number of service pilots, test pilots and design personnel. They reached a number of conclusions, most of which were to be rapidly promulgated, the most fundamental being that the Il-2 must have provisions of a rear defensive position. This was now considered vital and Stalin decreed that the conversion of the single seat version to the two seat variant should be accomplished in the shortest possible time, but without any interruption of Il-2 production.

During the Spring of 1942, the Ilyushin Design Bureau developed two variants of a two seat Il-2. The first variant was equipped with a MV-3 turret containing a Berezin UBT 12.7MM machine gun. Flight tests quickly revealed that the weight of the turret considerable reduced the aircraft's overall performance and, due to the fact that the turret shifted the center of gravity to the rear, the flight characteristics also were adversely affected and now were considered as unacceptable for a combat pilot with average flight skills.

The second variant was a nearly direct copy of the Il-2M-82 rear gun configuration. The cockpit was extended further back, with protective armor for the rear gunner added to both sides of the fuselage, so that the gunner sat in an armored "bathtub". In addition, the two side windows of the front canopy were slightly enlarged. In addition to the Berezin UBT 12.7MM

This experimental Il-2M had the cockpit armored capsule extended to the rear to make a rear gunner's position. The fuselage fuel tank was deleted and replaced by two wing tanks mounted in the underwing bomb bays. This conversion was not cleared for production. (Viktor Kulikov)

Fuselage Development

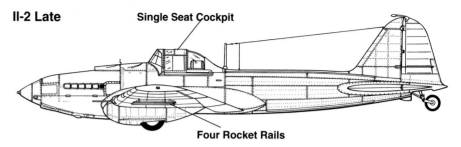

Il-2 Late — Single Seat Cockpit — Four Rocket Rails

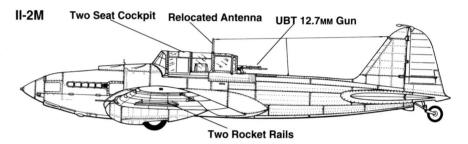

Il-2M — Two Seat Cockpit — Relocated Antenna — UBT 12.7MM Gun — Two Rocket Rails

machine gun, the gunner was equipped with a Type DA 7.62MM gun to engage ground targets or enemy aircraft approaching from the sides. The rear fuselage fuel tank was deleted and replaced by two armored fuel tanks which were installed in two of the wing bomb bays. As a result, only two bomb bays remained for ordnance. The problem of a reduced bomb load was one of the main reasons that this version was not accepted for production.

From the manufacturing point of view, both versions could not be easily placed into production since they required a number of changes. These changes could not be accomplished and still meet Stalin's condition that the introduction of the two seat version of the Il-2 could not interrupt Il-2 production output.

Production Il-2M

In March of 1942, the Ilyushin OKB converted a standard production Il-2 single seat aircraft into a two seat configuration, making only minimal changes to the aircraft's structure.

First, a mounting for a Berezin UBT 12.7MM machine gun was installed on the armor plate that separated the fuel tank from the cockpit. Then the rear glazed canopy of the single seat Il-2 was cut off to make room for the rear gunner compartment. As a result, the rear gun position was very small, cramped and primitive. The gunner was seated on a padded canvas seat suspended from either side of the cockpit walls. He was protected against fire from the rear hemisphere by a 6MM armored bulkhead in the rear fuselage.

When compared with the single seat Il-2, the gross weight on the Il-2M was raised by some 2,094 pounds (950 kg). This figure included the UBT gun, ammunition, additional armor protection and the gunner. Most of the weight was placed just behind the center of gravity and, as a result, the aircraft's stability was marginal and the handling characteristics were barely acceptable.

Regardless of these serious problems, the Il-2M passed State Acceptance Trials in the late Summer of 1942 and then the new type was immediately cleared for production by the Commissariat of Aviation Industry in September of 1942.

Other changes in the Il-2M included replacement of the long radio mast of the Il-2 with a small mast fitted on the rear canopy framing. In order to reduce weight, the Il-2M carried two instead of four underwing rocket rails. The external front sight of the PBP-1 gun sight, carried on top of the air intake, was replaced by an external front sight for the VV-1 gun sight which was mounted further the rear. The rudimentary VV-1 gun sight consisted of three aiming circles in the "diamond shaped" armor glass windscreen.

The ailerons balance weights were deleted on all two seat versions and the sand filter fitted to a small number of single seat Il-2s was standard on the Il-2M and subsequent variants. Some features, introduced on all two seaters, were also incorporated on a number of late production single seaters and are not totally unique to the Il-2M.

After thirty Il-2Ms were built, the side armor protection for the pilot and, especially for the gunner, was improved, although externally this modifications could not be detected. Even with this change, the armor protection of the rear gunner remained inadequate during the entire production life of the Il-2. Since the series production Il-2 had been originally designed as a single seater, it was impossible to enlarge the armored capsule further so that the gunner could also enjoyed the benefit of sufficient armor protection. This was due to the fact that such redesign work could not easily be absorbed into the production line without interrupting

Il-2M Rear Gun Position

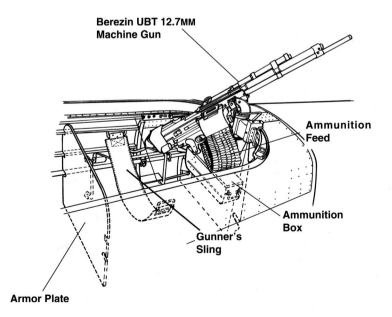

Berezin UBT 12.7ᴍᴍ Machine Gun

Ammunition Feed

Ammunition Box

Gunner's Sling

Armor Plate

This early Il-2M, Yellow 7, was shot down by Luftwaffe fighters and crash landed in an open field in German held territory. The aircraft was camouflaged with Black-Green and Olive Drab uppersurfaces and had a White fin tip. (Manfred Griehl)

production.

While all single seat Il-2s and the first production batches of Il-2Ms were equipped with the eleven foot diameter (3.4 meter) VISh-22T propeller, most of the later Il-2Ms and all subsequent versions, were equipped with a twelve foot (3.60 meter) AV-5L-158 propeller.

The Il-2M received its baptism of fire on 30 October 1942 during an attack on enemy airfields near Smolensk on the Central Front. During these early operational sorties, Il-2M gunners were credited with downing seven Messerschmitt Bf 109 fighters. The Messerschmitt pilots had presumably been taken unawares by the newly introduced rear gun position.

The rear gunner position had a dramatic boost in the combat effectiveness of the Assault Aviation Regiments. The Il-2M had not only a rear defense, but a second set of eyes to warn the pilot of fighter attacks coming from the rear, so that evasive action could be taken in time. Il-2M gunners were sometimes quite successful - if they survived long enough to become an ace. Rear gunner A. Karamshakov was credited with seven kills during 189 combat missions. Rear gunner N. Turbin claimed five kills, although two of them were shared kills. During his first mission, Sergeant N. Ryaboshapko of the 299th Assault Aviation Regiment, succeeded in shooting down a Focke Wulf Fw 189 twin engined reconnaissance aircraft. But the lack of adequate armor protection cost the lives of hundreds of rear gunners. Statistics show that during the Great Patriotic War seven gunners lost their lives for every pilot killed in action. A number of Assault Aviation Regiments had female rear gunners, such as the 804th Assault Aviation Regiment which served on the Kalinin front in May of 1943 .

The two seat Il-2M seldom flew above 3200 feet (1,000 meters) above ground level on combat missions. They would usually dive on their targets from 2,300 feet (700 meters) to about 1,300 feet (400 meters) in good weather. But, in bad weather and low clouds, attacks took place at altitudes of 65 to 160 feet (20 to 50 meters).

The element of surprise for the rear gunners did not last long and Luftwaffe fighter pilots

An early Il-2M, White 24, of the Black Sea Fleet. The White inscription on the fuselage reads "For the Fatherland." The arrow was in White and the aircraft was camouflage with Black-Green and Olive Drab uppersurfaces over Light Blue undersurfaces. (G. F. Petrov)

This Il-2M suffered battle damage to the starboard wing. The aircraft was returned to the Flight Research Institute at Zhukovsky during 1943 for testing. No national markings were ever carried on the wing uppersurfaces of any Il-2 variants. The paint has been worn off the port wingroot, which is where the crew normally boarded the aircraft. (Ivan Ivanov)

quickly developed tactics to counter the rear gun. Casualties among gunners soon reached alarming proportions and it became evident that, once the gunner was silenced, the Il-2M presented an even easier target than its single-seat predecessor. Using explosive ammunition, Luftwaffe fighter pilots attacked in a narrow arc immediately behind the tail of the Il-2M, which was not covered by the rear gun, either concentrating on the vulnerable wooden tail section and control surfaces, which disintegrated rapidly, or endeavoring to silence the gunner. Once silenced, they could attack at leisure from aft and above.

Experienced pilots could fly advanced aerobatics in the Il-2M and could engage in one-vs-one dogfights with enemy fighters but, unfortunately, most rudimentary trained Stormovik pilots were not aware of the maneuverability of their aircraft and none were trained in air combat skills or defensive combat flying techniques. Many of the new pilots arrived at the front with just ten hours of type experience and became easy prey for Luftwaffe fighter pilots, which enjoyed, at the time the two seat Il-2M entered combat, much better training in combat tactics.

Based on the combat experiences, the VUB-3 gun mount post was developed which increased the 12.7MM machine guns angle of fire to 45 degrees elevation, 12 degrees depresion and 35 degrees deflection. Initially the ammunition supply of the Il-2M was some 200 rounds; however, to save weight, this was later reduced to only 150 rounds.

Late production batches of Il-2Ms, built in late 1942, shortly before the production was switched to the Il-2 Type 3, were modified to give the gunner a glazed rear canopy to protect him from the elements. Often, this rear glazing was removed in the field, since it cut down on the gunner's field of view.

The Il-2M was regarded as an interim two seat variant, which was quickly developed to give the Assault Aviation Regiments a rear defense in the shortest possible time.

A Il-2M, White 24, of the Black Sea FLeet, Soviet Naval Aviation, prepares to taxi out on another mission. The inscription on the fuselage side reads, *For the honor of the Guard!* The three small Red stars on the fin are for air-to-air victories, although it is not known it the kills were scored by the pilot or by the gunner. (Carl-Fredrik Geust)

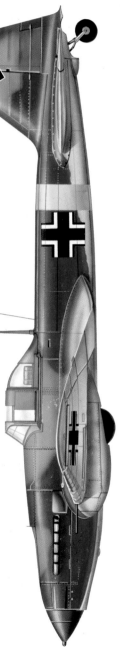

This early production Il-2 was captured by the Luftwaffe and repainted with German markings including the Yellow identification bands carried by Luftwaffe aircraft operating on the Eastern Front.

This Il-2, Yellow 3, was modified in the field with external stiffeners on the rear fuselage. The inscription reads "For Otradnov" and refers to a fellow pilot killed in combat.

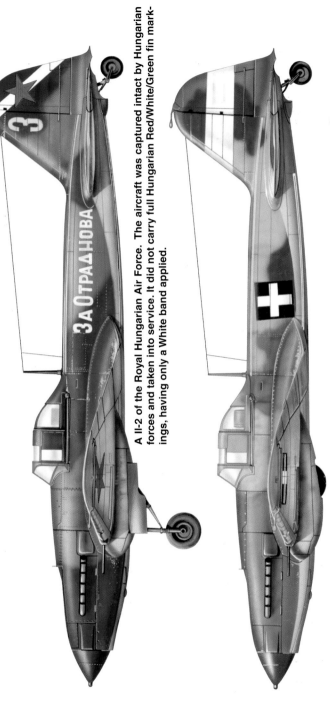

A Il-2 of the Royal Hungarian Air Force. The aircraft was captured intact by Hungarian forces and taken into service. It did not carry full Hungarian Red/White/Green fin markings, having only a White band applied.

This Il-2M was assigned to the Black Sea Fleet. The inscription reads, "For the honor of the Guard!" It carried three Red star kill markings on the fin above the national insignia.

A Il-2 Type 3 of the 281st Assault Aviation Division, 14th Air Army. The aircraft carried a small Red heart on the fin. This type of personal marking was unusual on Il-2s.

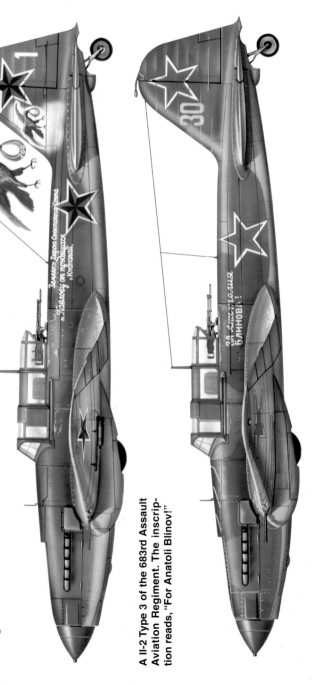

White 1, a Il-2 Type 3, was flown by twice Hero of the Soviet Union Ivan F. Pavlov. The inscription reads, "To the compatriot Hero of the Soviet Union comrade Pavlov from the workers of the city of Kustanaj." The aircraft was assigned to the 6th Guards Assault Aviation Regiment.

A Il-2 Type 3 of the 683rd Assault Aviation Regiment. The inscription reads, "For Anatoli Blinov!"

This Yugoslav Air Force Il-2 Type 3, White 14, was flown as a night bomber during 1949. A coat of Dark Gray camouflage paint was applied over the original Soviet colors.

This Czech-built B-33 was flown by the Polish Air Force during late 1957. The aircraft was assigned to the 30th Naval Aviation Regiment and was lost on 24 May 1957.

This Il-10 of the North Korean Peoples Air Force was captured by Marines and returned to the U.S. for testing.

Some late production Il-2Ms, as well as early production Il-2 Type 3s had a portion of the rear canopy glazing cut back in order to improve the gunner's view. Such field modifications were common among Assault Aviation Regiments, as crews sought to improve their aircraft. (Ivan Ivanov)

(Right) Ground crews prepare a Il-2M for a mission during late 1943. The aircraft is unusual in that it carries two tactical numbers, White 12 on the fin and Yellow 36 on the rear fuselage. The national markings on the fin, fuselage and the wing undersurfaces had a thick White border with a thin Red outline. (G.F. Petrov)

The Stormovik could absorb a lot of battle damage and still bring its crew home. This Il-2M, Yellow 5, has had the port elevator nearly shot away and there is severe damage to the port wing root as well. The aircraft was camouflaged Black-Green and Olive Drab with a Red arrow on the fuselage. (G.F. Petrov)

These factory fresh Il-2Ms carry overall White Winter camouflage. They were purchased from funds collected by the *All Union Leninist Youth Organization of Yaroslav* and were being turned over to front-line. The inscription on the fuselage identifies the donors, *Yaroslavskij Komsomolez* (*All Union Leninist Youth Organization of Yaroslav*) and is in Red. (SHAA/B84-801)

27

This Black-Green and Olive Drab Il-2M was lifted by ground crews so that the starboard landing gear could be lowered and locked down. The only visible damage was a bent wing tip and bent back propeller blades indicating that the engine was still running when the landing gear failed. (G. F. Petrov)

The Il-2M and the later Il-2 Type 3 were equipped with a very rudimentary VV-1 gun sight, which replaced the earlier PBP-I gun sight. Three aiming circles were painted on the diamond shaped armor glass windshield. Cockpit instrumentation included a type BE-499 fuel gauge, a TVE-41 water temperature gauge, a TE-22 RPM indicator, a KI-11 compass, a AGP-I artificial horizon, a RPK-10 position indicator and a Pioneer copy of a turn and bank indicator. (Hannu Valtonen)

A camouflaged Il-2M, Yellow 6, prepares for another mission during late 1943. This aircraft has had only a portion of the rear fuselage and part of the wings coated with a temporary White Winter camouflage finish. (G.F. Petrov)

Il-2 Type 3

Throughout its production life, Stormovik pilots complained that the Il-2 was a sluggish and unresponsive aircraft with poor stability. The last problem had been compounded with the introduction of the interim Il-2M two seater. Stalin's directive forbade introduction of any modifications that were likely to disrupt deliveries of Il-2s to the front and, as a result, Ilyushin could do little more than make small changes, but the dangerous stability problems of the Il-2M demanded particular attention, This problem resulted in the introduction of the Il-2 Type 3, which was considered the definitive two-seater and was to become numerically the most important variant of the basic design.

Partly as a result of wind tunnel research of the Central Aero and Hydrodynamics Institute at Zhukovsky, the outer wing panels of the Il-2 were given a 15 degree sweep back which transferred lift rearward, compensating for the rear shift of the center of gravity, which had accented the Il-2's worst characteristics.

The State Acceptance Trials of the Il-2 Type 3 were completed on 12 December 1942, and the new swept back wing was quickly put into production, replacing the original wing.

Apart from the new wing, the Il-2 Type 3s leaving the assembly lines during late 1942 and early 1943 were identical to late production Il-2Ms. As quickly as they came off the assembly line, Il-2 Type 3s were rushed into combat in the Stalingrad area.

While the first production batches of Il-2 Type 3s were equipped with the standard 1,600 hp AM-38 power plant, aircraft produced from January 1943 onward were modified with the 1,700 hp AM-38F power plant (the suffix "F" in the engine designation stood for *Forsirovannie* or boosted). The AM-38F ran at a lower compression ratio than the AM-38 (from 7.0 to 6.0) and, as a result, the engine could burn low-octane fuel, like that used for military trucks. The additional power improved the overall performance of the Il-2 Type 3. Externally there was no difference between the cowling of the AM-38 and AM-38F powered aircraft.

Wind tunnel research by the Central Aero and Hydrodynamics Institute at Zhukovsky was performed on this pre-production Il-2 Type 3. As a result, a 15 degree sweep back was added to the outer wing panels, transferring lift rearward and compensating for the aft movement of the center of gravity. (G.F. Petrov)

Fuselage Development

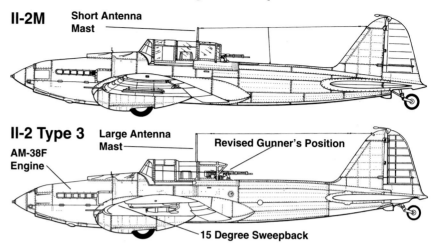

Il-2M Short Antenna Mast

Il-2 Type 3 Large Antenna Mast
AM-38F Engine
Revised Gunner's Position
15 Degree Sweepback

During the production life of the Il-2 Type 3, a number of modifications were introduced to the basic airframe. The starboard pitot tube was moved from a position near the VYa-23 23MM cannon to a position close to the wing tip late production Il-2 Type 3s.

The early Il-2 Type 3 had two under wing rocket rails identical to those used on the Il-2M. These rails were attached by two mounts to the wing. Later Il-2 Type 3s were modified with a new rocket rail which had a fairing covering the rail.

The rear canopy for the gunner was also modified. The first Il-2 Type 3 had the same canopy as the late production Il-2M. Later Il-2 Type 3s had a semi-circular rear canopy section which was introduced during the Spring of 1943 (some Il-2 Type 3s were seen with this section removed as a field modification). For a short period, these Il-2 Type 3s continued to use the small radio mast fitted on the rear of the canopy frame, but most late production Il-2 Type 3s were modified with a long antenna mast mounted in the same location (some late aircraft had the antenna moved to a position on the pilots canopy framing). Late production Il-2

Static tests were performed on an engineless Il-2 Type 3 at the Central Aero and Hydrodynamics Institute at Zhukovsky. The hole in the starboard wing root is where the sand air filter would normally be located. (G.F. Petrov)

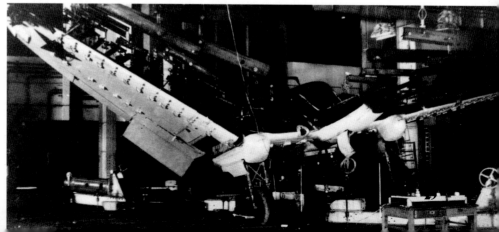

Early production Il-2 Type 3s undergo final assembly at State Aircraft Factory 18 at Kuibyshev during early 1943. This nearly completed Il-2 Type 3 has two rocket rails under the wing instead of the four carried by the single seat Il-2. The open doors under the wings are the bomb bay doors for the wing bomb bays. (G. F. Petrov)

Type 3s also had a ventilation hatch on the port gunners canopy.

A number of Assault Aviation Regiments removed the entire rear canopy of the gunner position as a field modification. This was basically done for two reasons; combat experience revealed that it was quite difficult to bail out from the gunner's position, especially when the canopy failed to open. The other basic reason was to improve the gunner's field of view. One test Il-2 Type 3 had a fully closed rear gunner's compartment. The side windows were enlarged, but this modification did not develop beyond the testing stage.

Most Il-2 Type 3s were equipped with a squared off cannon barrel fairing, although the last production batches of the Il-2 Type 3 had a triangle shaped cannon barrel fairing.

A number of tail wheel fairings were introduced on the Il-2 Type. Most early production Il-2 Type 3s were fitted with a medium size covering, while the majority of Il-2 Type 3 were fitted with a shorter fairing. Some Il-2 Type 3s also received a longer fairing.

The Il-2 became, numerically, the most important aircraft of the Red Air Force. In 1942, it represented one third of the entire inventory. In the Summer of 1942, some 1,000 Il-2s were being produced monthly. In early 1944, the Stormovik still represented one third of the opera-

Newly completed Il-2 Type 3s are parked on the ramp at State Aircraft Factory 18, awaiting final acceptance flights during in early 1943. All of the aircraft were camouflaged in Black-Green and Olive Drab. The early Il-2 Type 3 had the pitot tube inboard on the wing, while late Il-2 Type 3s had the pitot tube located outboard on the wing. (G. F. Petrov)

Private Anna Petrova Bogdanova of the 804th ShAP checks her Berezin UBT 12.7MM heavy machine gun prior to a mission. The unit was based at an advance airfield on the Kalinin front during May of 1943. (Ivan Ivanov)

tional strength of the Red Air Force.

In the second half of the war the supply of raw materials gradually got better and, as a result, the wooden wing was replaced by a metal wing in production batches delivered during the Autumn of 1944. Some late Il-2 Type 3s, produced early in1945, had the rear wooden fuselage and the tail also replaced by an all metal structure.

Cockpit instrumentation was very rudimentary and included a type BE-499 fuel gauge, a TVE-41 water temperature gauge, a type TE-22 RPM indicator, a KI-11 compass, a type AGP-1 artificial horizon, a RPK-10 position indicator and a Pioneer copy of a turn and bank

Rockets

RS-82 Rocket

Electrical
Connection

Rocket Rail
Mounts

Type RO Rocket Rail

RS-132 Rocket

Type RO Rocket Rail

Private Klavdija Yefimovna Danilova of the 3rd Squadron, 6th Guards Assault Aviation Regiment, loads 23ᴍᴍ rounds into the ammunition bay of the VYa-23 23ᴍᴍ cannon of an early Il-2 Type 3 on 24 July 1943. These rounds could penetrate armor up to 25ᴍᴍ thick at distances up to 1,300 feet (400 meters). Each ammunition bay could hold up to 300 rounds. (Ivan Ivanov)

Wing Development

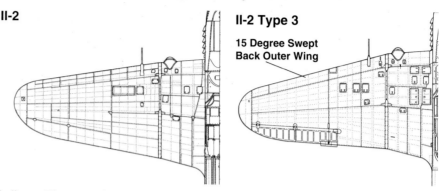

Il-2

Il-2 Type 3

15 Degree Swept Back Outer Wing

indicator. There were lamps mounted in the front cockpit to allow the pilot to read maps during hours of darkness.

During the Great Patriotic War, a number of new weapons were introduced. One of the most successful was the PTAB hollow charge anti-tank bomb. This weapon weighed 2.5 pounds and 192 of them could be housed in a KMB canister. One KMB canister could be carried in each of the four bomb bays in the wing. Tests, with this weapon, proved so successful that Colonel General Boris L. Vanikov, the People's Commissar for Armament, ordered that 8,000 units be produced by 15 May 1943.

The PTAB was used for the first time on a large scale during the Battle of Kursk in the Orjol - Kursk sector in July of 1943. The new weapon proved to be extremely successful, with the bombs penetrating up to 70ᴍᴍ of armor. When the tank's gasoline tanks were ignited, the shock wave, from the resulting explosion, and fragments of armor hit the crew and ammunition, which usually exploded.

On 2 July 1943 a group of eight Il-2 Type 3s of the 504th Assault Aviation Regiment of the 1st Guards Assault Aviation Division (formerly the 226th Assault Aviation Division), assigned to the 8th Air Army under the command of Hero of the Soviet Union, Captain M.I. Smilskij attacked an concentration of about seventy German tanks poised for a counterattack. The Il-2s made five runs, dropping no less than 1,232 PTAB hollow charge anti-tank bombs. They set fifteen enemy vehicles afire.

On 5 July 1943, Il-2s of the 291st Assault Aviation Division of the 16th Air Army, under the command of Colonel A. Vitruk, claimed the destruction of thirty tanks with these bombs near Voronezh. Usually, PTAB hollow charge anti-tank bombs were released from an altitude of 230-330 feet (70 meters to 100 meters) above the battlefield and covered an area about 50 feet (15 meters) wide and 230 feet (70 meters) long. During the battle of Kursk, the 16th Air Army, under the command of Colonel General S.I. Rudenko, flew no less than 56,350 combat sorties, the most flown by Il-2s.

During 1942, the improved RBS-82 and RBS-132 rockets were introduced into service. These were developed from the earlier RS-82 and the RS-132 rockets. These were equipped with an armor piercing warhead and a more powerful rocket engine for use against tanks and armored vehicles.

One method, used to discourage the fighter attacks from the blind spot behind the tail was the installation of a DAG-10 grenade launcher in the rear fuselage. The launcher held ten

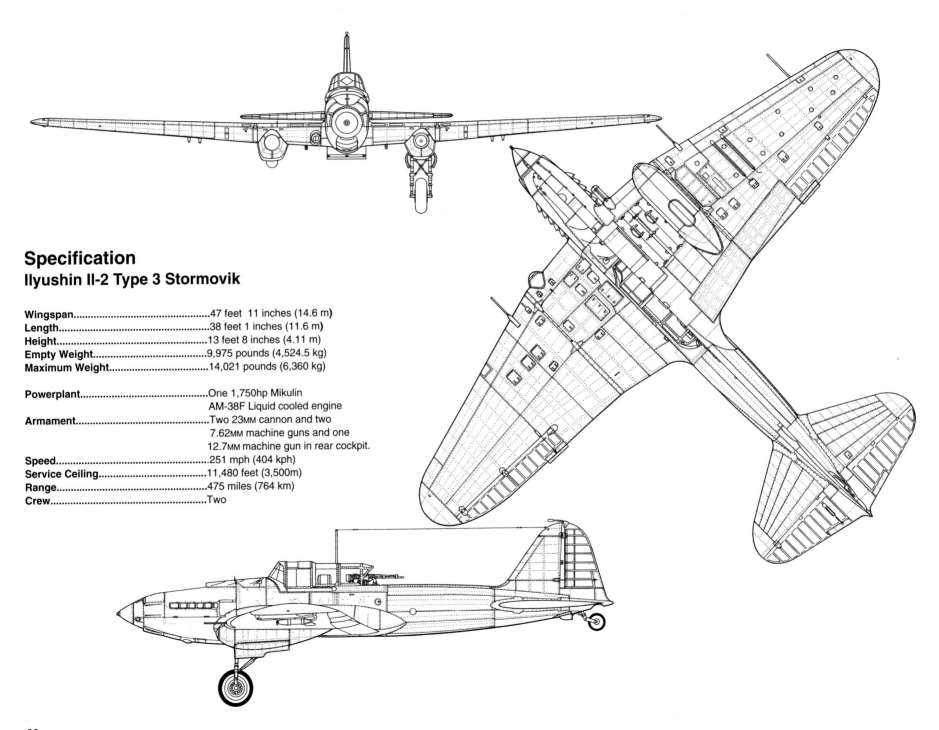

Specification
Ilyushin Il-2 Type 3 Stormovik

Wingspan	47 feet 11 inches (14.6 m)
Length	38 feet 1 inches (11.6 m)
Height	13 feet 8 inches (4.11 m)
Empty Weight	9,975 pounds (4,524.5 kg)
Maximum Weight	14,021 pounds (6,360 kg)
Powerplant	One 1,750hp Mikulin AM-38F Liquid cooled engine
Armament	Two 23mm cannon and two 7.62mm machine guns and one 12.7mm machine gun in rear cockpit.
Speed	251 mph (404 kph)
Service Ceiling	11,480 feet (3,500m)
Range	475 miles (764 km)
Crew	Two

These Il-2 Type 3s have enlarged rear cockpit canopies which were used on most Type 3s, although they still carry short antenna masts. The tactical number, White 75, was very crudely applied to the second aircraft. (G.F. Petrov)

grenades and could be operated by either the pilot or gunner. The grenades were attached to small parachutes which opened automatically. They were set with a three-second fuses so that they exploded about 328 feet (100 meters) to the rear of the aircraft and in the path of the pursing fighters.

Reduced losses were also achieved by a change of tactics. Enroute to a target area, Stormoviks usually flew at very low altitudes in a "V" or echelon formation which ensured the greatest volume of defensive fire. For repelling fighter attacks over enemy occupied territory, the formation reformed into a "circle." The crews covering one another with their cannons and machine guns.

The Il-2 could take a lot of punishment and still bring the crew home safely. A study of the actions of Assault Aviation Regiments of the 3rd Air Army, under the command of Colonel General N.F. Papavin, revealed that for the second half of the Great Patriotic War, when the 3rd Air Army took part in the Belorussian campaign and later struck into East Prussia, fifty percent of the Il-2s returned from a mission with some battle damage, but only 2.8 percent of the Stormovik were actually lost. Six percent of the crippled Il-2s had to make crash landings, but some ninety percent of the damaged Il-2s could be repaired at the front with the help of specialists assigned to each Assault Aviation Regiment. Only ten percent had to be shipped back to Repair Depots in the rear or had to be scrapped.

A line-up of Il-2 Type 3s of the 281st Assault Aviation Division, 14th Air Army. The aircraft in the foreground, has the tactical number, White 17, on the tail and the number, White 66, on the rear fuselage. The aircraft carries a Red heart on the fin with a thin White outline. This aircraft lacks the ventilation hatch on the rear canopy which was standard on most Il-2 Type 3s with this canopy configuration. (Klaus Niska via Carl-Fredrik Geust)

This Il-2 Type 3, White 63, is camouflaged in Black-Green and Olive Drab. The national marking is carried on the fin, but not on the rear fuselage. The White lettering above the star on the fin are the aircraft's serial numbers. (Carl-Fredrik Geust)

The average number of missions performed by Il-2s during the entire Great Patriotic War was thirty sorties before the aircraft was lost. In the early stage of the war, this figure was dramatically lower. For more than half of the war, the Il-2 pilots could not count on fighter escorts; however, the situation became better in the final months of the war, when enough Fighter Aviation Regiments were available to protect the Il-2s from enemy fighters. One third of all airmen who received the country's highest award, the Hero of the Soviet Union, were Stormovik crews.

Early Il-2 Type 3s left the factory in the Black-Green and Olive-Drab uppersurface camouflage. Later production batches were delivered in a camouflage of Earth Brown and Medium Green on the uppersurfaces with Light Blue undersurfaces. Most Il-2 Type 3s had the national markings on the wing undersurfaces, the rear fuselage and the fin. Initially the national markings had a thin Black or White outline. During late 1943, the national markings were changed with a thick White border and thin Red outline. A number of Il-2 Type 3s did not carry the national markings on the fuselage. Some of the Guard regiments had a "Kremlin" style star national marking painted on the fuselage and fin. The tactical number, normally a two digit number, was carried either on the rudder or on the fuselage, depending on the Regiment.

When production of the Il-2 ended, a total of 36,163 Il-2s had been delivered to the front. No other combat aircraft in the Second World War, of any nation, had been produced in equal quantities.

During mid-1955, the North Atlantic Treaty Organization (NATO) introduced the ASCC-Reporting Name System. Although at that time there were no Il-2 Type 3s remaining in front line service, NATO still assigned the aircraft the code name Bark.

Tail Wheel Fairing Variations

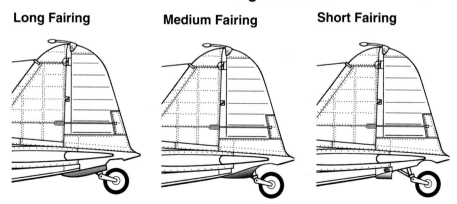

Long Fairing   **Medium Fairing**   **Short Fairing**

This Olive Drab and Earth Brown Il-2 Type 3, Red 12, carries a "Kremlin" style star on the rear fuselage, while the fin and underwing markings are standard stars with White borders and thin Red outlines. (Ivan Ivanov)

Ground crews perform an engine overhaul on a Il-2 Type 3 at Pancevo air base near Belgrade. The aircraft is unusual in that it has no tactical number. This Il-2 belongs to one of the few Assault Aviation Regiments that operated from Yugoslav territory during the Winter of 1944. (Milan Micevski)

A few late production Il-2 Type 3s had the antenna mast fitted on the front cockpit canopy frame. This Il-2 Type 3, Yellow 22, shares a muddy airfield with some Lavochkin La-5FN fighters which served as the Stormovik's escort. (SHAA/B79 2254)

Gunner Gennady I. Mamachrin, of the 6th Guards Assault Aviation Regiment, man's the gunner's position of a Il-2 Type 3. His pilot was Ivan F. Pavlov, twice Hero of the Soviet Union. During January of 1945, the unit was attached to the 1st Baltic Front. The aircraft was purchased with funds collected by the workers of the city of Kustanaj. Most Il-2 Type 3s with the extended rear gunner's canopy, had a ventilation hatch on the port side, which could be opened by the gunner in flight. (Ivan Ivanov)

ivan F. Pavlov, twice Hero of the Soviet Union, poses in front of his Il-2 Type 3 on 16 January 1945. Pavlov flew a total of 204 missions during the war. The inscription reads, *To the compatriot Hero of the Soviet Union, comrade Pavlov from the workers of the city of Kustanaj.* His gunner, Gunner Gennady I. Mamachrin, was credited with the destruction of a Fw-190. (Ivan Ivanov)

This experimental Il-2 Type 3 had a fully enclosed rear gunner's position and enlarged side windows. This version never progressed beyond the test stage and was not put into production. (Robert Bock)

Private Yekaterina P. Butorina, of the 6th Assault Aviation Regiment, loads RS-82 rockets onto the Type RO underwing rocket rails of a Il-2 Type 3 during August of 1943. The unfaired rocket rails identify this as an early production Type 3. (Ivan Ivanov)

(Right) A late production Il-2 Type 3 parked on the grass at a forward field during a stopover on the ferry flight from State Aircraft Factory 18 to the front. The aircraft is fitted with late style RO rocket rails that are equipped with a fairing around the rail. (Viktor Kulikov)

A pre-flight briefing for Stormovik pilots of the 6th Guards Assault Aviation Regiment on 6 March 1945. The aircraft in the background is a Il-2 Type 3, Red 17, with its canopy covered by a protective canvas covering. (Ivan Ivanov)

V.I. Mychlik was the commander of the 566th Assault Aviation Regiment, 227th Assault Aviation Division of the 13th Air Army. The inscription on his Il-2 Type 3, White 07, reads "For Leningrad." The 13th Air Army was responsible for the air assaults that helped break the 870 day siege of Leningrad. (Ivan Ivanov)

Il-2T Torpedo Bomber

During the Great Patriotic War, a large number of Il-2 Type 3s were assigned to Soviet Naval Aviation, which used the same combat tactics as the Red Air Force. Naval Il-2 pilots developed the so called "Frog" technique for attacking enemy vessels at sea. The Il-2 approached the target at an altitude of 100 feet (30 meters) and at a speed of 250 mph (400 km/h), then climbed immediately ahead of the target and released their bombs. Of the four FAB 100 general purpose bombs, released against a ship, one bomb would usually hit the ship. Soviet Naval Aviation Il-2 units took part in land offensives such as the campaigns to expel Germans from Belorussia and the Crimea.

The Il-2T was a modification for Soviet Naval Aviation which allowed the Il-2 to carry a Type 45-12-AN torpedo on a crutch under the fuselage. The torpedo had to be dropped from very low levels. Most Il-2Ts were assigned to the Black Sea Fleet of the Soviet Naval Aviation. This variant of the Il-2 Type 3 was built in very limited numbers.

Il-2KR

The Il-2KR was developed to serve as a spotter aircraft to control artillery fire. The first Il-2KRs were delivered in the Summer of 1943. With the exception of the Berezin UBT 12.7MM gun, which was replaced by an AFA-1 or AFA-1M camera, the armament remained unchanged.

The AFA-1 camera, as well as its successor, the AFA-1M, was installed on the same gun mount as the Berezin UBT machine gun. The camera weighed 45 pounds (20.6 kg) and two different focal length lens could be used, either a 300MM or 500MM. During a mission, up to 150 7x7 inch (18X18 cm) negatives could be exposed. The pictures were taken with the help of an electrical motor and the observer could take them remotely with the use of a cable release in the rear cockpit. The antenna mast on the Il-2KR was moved from the rear canopy frame to a position on top of the front cockpit frame. A RSB-bis (*Radiostancija dlja bombardirovotshnych*/Radio Station for Bomber) radio was installed in the fuselage behind the pilot's armored head rest. In order to make room for the radio the fuselage fuel tank was slightly reduced in size.

The RSB-bis was used for communications between the Il-2KR and the ground control post directing the artillery fire. The RSB-bis transmitter unit weighed 30 pounds (13.5 kg) and used four different frequency bands. It was powered by a RUK-300A generator. The Type US receiver weighed 12 pounds (5.5 kg) and operated on five different frequency bands. The Type US receiver was powered by a RU-11A generator.

The Il-2KR served as an aerial observation post for the direction of artillery fire at the front. The AFA-I aerial camera replaced the UBT 12.7MM heavy machine gun in the rear cockpit. A RSI-bis radio, usually carried by bombers, was used for communications between the Il-2KR and the ground commander. The radio antenna mast was relocated to the front canopy frame. (G.F. Petrov)

Foreign Il-2s

Poland

Poland, together with Yugoslavia, was by far the largest operator of the Il-2 during and after the Second World War. Polish Stormovik pilots were checked in the Il-2 after graduating from the 9th and 10th Military Air School at Chkalov. The gunners were trained at the 87th Rear Gunner School at Grechovka. Due to the length of their training cycle, the first group of Polish air crews were not fully operational until August of 1944.

The 611th Assault Aviation Regiment, equipped with thirty-two Il-2 Type 3s and a single Polikarpov Po-2 was the first operational Polish Il-2 unit. The 611th Assault Aviation Regiment became the 8th Assault Aviation Wing in the 1st Air Division of the Soviet sponsored Polish Air Force and saw action for the first time on 23 August 1944, attacking enemy artillery positions at Mazovsk near Warsaw.

The Polish Il-2 Type 3s of the 3rd Assault Aviation Wing supported the uprising in Warsaw by attacking German artillery positions in the Polish capital. The unit also operated in the north and north-western areas of Warsaw. On 19 January 1945 formations of the 3rd Assault Aviation Wing performed a fly-by over the liberated Polish capital.

In February 1945, Polish Il-2s saw action in the Pomorze (Pomerania) area and attacked targets in Chojnice, Szczecinek, Barwice, Zlocienice and Czaplinek Kamienice. Then they moved into the Pila and Poznan areas of Poland. In March of 1945, Polish Il-2 formations

During the war, Polish Il-2 Type 3s carried the Polish chessboard national marking on the nose, in addition to standard Soviet Air Force markings. Some aircraft carried the chessboard ahead of the exhaust stacks, while others carried the marking behind the exhausts. (Andrzej Morgala)

This Polish Air Force Il-2 Type 3 has the radio mast relocated to the front canopy frame. The spinner was painted White, while the forward portion of the landing gear fairing was in Red. (Andrzej Morgala)

were used to attack the so called Pomerania Line, a German defensive line against the Red Army in Pomerania and took part in the liberation of the Kolobrzeg harbor from elements of the German Army.

Between 19 March and 8 April 1945 the Polish units flew a number of observation flights over the Baltic sea and occasionally attacked targets, such as the V-2 missile launching site near Kamien Pomorski. From 16 April 1945 the 3rd Assault Aviation Wing launched its last offensive on the Oder River and took part in the battle of Berlin.

The 2nd Air Division of Polish Air Force was formed at Volchansk on 30 September 1944 and included the 658th, 382nd and 384th Assault Aviation Regiments, which were renumbered the 6th, 7th and 8th Assault Aviation Wings. In early April of 1945, these formations flew from the Ukraine to Poland and saw action in the final days of the war, including the capture of Berlin by the Red Army. On 29 April 1945, the Polish Il-2s, escorted by Yak-9s of the 10th Fighter Aviation Regiment, attacked the major Luftwaffe air base at Neuruppin.

The Polish Il-2 units were credited with the destruction of twenty-five tanks, 1,300 vehicles, 290 pieces of rolling stock, twenty-eight locomotives and 400 anti-aircraft and artillery positions. At the end of the Second World War, the Polish Air Force had 158 Il-2 Type 3s and fifteen Il-2UTs in their inventory.

Polish Il-2 Type 3s carried a large Red/White chessboard, the Polish national marking, painted on the nose, either under the exhaust stacks or immediately behind the exhaust stacks. This was in addition to standard Soviet Air Force national and tactical markings. After they were absorbed in the newly formed Polish Air Force the Red star was replaced by the Polish national marking on the wing and fuselage, but after a brief period, the chessboard on the nose was overpainted.

After the war, a number of Polish Il-2 Type 3s were fitted with a direction finding loop antenna on the rear fuselage for a RPKO-10M radio compass. A few Polish Il-2s had the bulged panel behind the exhaust stacks replaced by a flat panel with five vents. A number of Polish Il-2 Type 3a also had the VV-1 gun sight replaced by the PBP-lB gun sight, which was also fitted to the Il-10 and the Yak-9D fighter. These modifications were unique to Polish post war Il-2 Type 3s.

On 1 October 1945, the Polish Air Force had a total of 202 Il-2 Type 3s including twenty-four Il-2UT trainers. In 1946 a number of early Polish Air Force Il-2 Type 3s were exchanged for late production Il-2 Type 3s with all-metal fuselage and wings.

Il-2 Type 3s of the Polish Air Force saw action after the end of the Second World War. The

A line up of Polish Air Force Il-2 Type 3s. All of the aircraft have the late style cannon fairing. The second aircraft in the row is equipped with a direction finder loop antenna for a RPK-10 radio compass. (Andrzej Morgala)

The VV-1 gun sight on some Polish Il-2 Type 3s was replaced by the more advanced PBP-1B gun sight, which was also used on the Yak-9D and Il-10. (Andrzej Morgala)

UPA (*Ukrajinska Povstantshiska Armija*/Ukraine Insurgent Army) fought against the Red Army after it re-entered the Ukraine in 1944 and carried out a civil war until some time in the 1950s. Four Polish Il-2 Type 3s of the 6th Assault Aviation Wing took part in the fighting against formations of the Ukraine Insurgent Army which were operating in East Poland during early May of 1947. The unit was based at Jasionka airfield near Rzeszow and flew their first mission on l0 June 1947. In late June, with the end of the fighting, the unit was withdrawn.

In September 1949, shortly before the remaining Il-2s were struck off charge, Poland still had 138 Il-2 Type 2s and thirty-two Il-2UTs in their inventory.

Yugoslavia

On 21 September 1944, the Yugoslav guerrilla leader and former general secretary of the Communist Party, Josip Broz Tito, who had been in close co-operation with the British, flew to Moscow to meet with Stalin, who promised him military assistance. Under this agreement, a number of Yugoslav pilots were trained in the Soviet Union, including some who were trained on the Il-2 Type 3.

During the capture of Belgrade between 28 September and 20 October 1944, formations of the 3rd Ukrainian Army, under the command of Marshall Fyodor I. Tolbuchin, were supported by Bulgarian and Yugoslav formations and a few Soviet Assault Aviation Regiments of the 17th Air Army and the 5th Air Army. Some of these units were based at Pancevo Air Field.

From December of 1944 to the Spring of 1945 Yugoslav pilots were also trained at the Yugoslavian Assault Aviation Training Center at Zemun Air Base near Belgrade by Soviet instructors. The 421st and 422nd Assault Aviation Regiments were totally manned by Yugoslav personnel. A large number of Yugoslav flown Il-2 Type 3s were destroyed in com-

bat and during accidents and Yugoslav Il-2 units suffered heavy losses during their operations in the Vojvodina area.

In Stalin's eyes, Yugoslavia had made a major contribution to the defeat of fascism and the first Soviet post war treaty of friendship, mutual aid and post-war collaboration with a new socialist country was signed with Marshall Tito during his visit Moscow in April of 1945. It was also agreed that the Soviet Union would give the Yugoslavs military assistance to form twelve army and two air divisions. A large contingent of Soviet military advisors worked in Yugoslavia while, in the USSR, thousands of Yugoslav military personnel underwent military training.

In the Summer of 1945, one Yugoslav manned Assault Aviation Regiment with forty Il-2 Type 3s, arrived from training in the Soviet Union. Also, in order to make up for wartime losses, the Yugoslav Air Force received a further thirty Il-2 Type 3s from the Soviet Union in the Autumn of 1945.

In 1947, an additional eighty Il-2 Type 3 were acquired. Fifty of these came from Bulgaria

A Il-2 Type 3 of the 422nd Assault Aviation Regiment, Yugoslav Air Force at Zagreb Air Base during May of 1945. The aircraft has a White spinner and fully faired underwing rocket rails. (Milan Micevski)

This Il-2 Type 3 was assigned to the 3rd Assault Aviation Regiment, Yugoslav Air Force during 1948. The original wooden rear fuselage was replaced by a Yugoslav manufactured all metal fuselage. The tactical number, Black 4077, was carried in small Black digits on the fin. (Milan Micevski)

This Il-2 Type 3. White 14, was used for night operations and had a coat of Black camouflage applied over the original paint. The tactical number, Black 4071, was repainted on the fin. The aircraft was taking part in maneuvers held in Yugoslavia during 1949. (Milan Micevski)

in March, while thirty were purchased directly from the Soviet Union in May. A total of 213 Il-2 Type 3s and Il-2UTs served with six Assault Aviation Regiments in the Yugoslav Air Force.

When Belgrade signed a Bulgarian - Yugoslav treaty of friendship and dispatched a Yugoslav Air Regiment to Albania without informing Stalin, the once warm Soviet - Yugoslav relationship became strained. A meeting of a Yugoslav delegation with Stalin on l0 February 1949 ended with no constructive agreements and resulted in the definitive break in Yugoslav - Soviet relations.

As a result, the Air Force established a number of measures in order to keep the Il-2 Type 3 fleet flying, since they were now cut off from spare parts from the Soviet Union. The Zemunkiy Ikar factory built 300 metal fuselages to replace the original wooden fuselages of the Il-2 Type 3s built during the war. About a dozen Il-2 Type 3s were also converted to two seat Il-2UT trainers.

A number of Il-2 Type 3 were repainted with a Black camouflage finish sprayed over their original paint and were used for night operations during 1949. Finally, in 1955 all remaining Il-2 Type 3s and Il-2UTs were withdrawn from operational service.

Czechoslovakia

On 24 September 1944 the first contingent of Czech airmen began conversion training in the Il-2 Type 3 as part of the 41st Advanced Training Aviation Regiment based at Przemysl airfield in Poland.

The training was so intensive and well organized that alread,y on 15 October 1944, a group of thirteen Il-2 Czech crews were selected to support the Slovakian insurgent forces at Tri Duby (Three Oaks), lying between Zvolen and Banska Bystrica. The insurgent army which numbered about 50,000 soldiers was commanded by Lieutenant Colonel Jan Golina. The ill fated Slovakian insurgent uprising; however, was suppressed by the Germans in late October 1944, before the Czech pilots could get into action and the Czech Il-2 mission was canceled by the 2nd Air Army under the command of Major General S.A. Krasovskij.

The training process proceeded relatively slowly, due to unfavorable weather, a temporary lack of aircraft and the unequal training levels of the Slovak pilots. The less experienced of them found it difficult to make the transition from obsolete biplanes to the Il-2 and this resulted in a number of accidents.

The lst Czechoslovak Independent Combined Air Division was officially formed on 25

January 1945, being subordinate to Lieutenant General N.V. Zhdanov, commander of the Soviet 8th Air Army. Over seventy percent of the unit were Slovak airmen. The 3rd Czechoslovak Battle Regiment, as part of the lst Czechoslovak Independent Combined Air Division, was equipped with thirty-four Il-2 Type 3s, some of which were late production variants with all metal wings and rear fuselages.

In the following weeks, the training of Czech pilots and gunners nearly came to a standstill, nevertheless the program continued at Przemysl, very slowly and sometimes interrupted by crashes and landing accidents. Between 20 February and 5 March 1945, the 3rd Czechoslovak Battle Regiment was based at Iwonicz airfield for further training. The unit was considered to be combat ready on 23 March 1945. But before the Regiment moved into combat, additional weapons training with RS-82 rockets and bombs was conducted.

Between 7 and 11 April 1945, the 3rd Czechoslovak Battle Regiment with its thirty-three Il-2 Type 3s and two Il-2UTs moved to a new base near Katowice in liberated Poland. After a short time it was discovered that the grass runway was too soft for the Il-2s and the unit moved to Poremba airfield, only twelve miles (twenty kilometers) from the front lines.

On 14 April 1945, the unit flew its first combat mission when a group of eight Il-2 Type 3s, escorted by nine Czech flown La-5FN fighters, took off to attack artillery positions and tank concentrations near the village of Olza. This mission was part of a Red Army offensive to drive the Germans from the heavily industrialized area of Ostrava in Czechoslovakia. The same target was attacked later the same day, but during take-off two Il-2s collided leaving only seven to proceed to the target.

A day later missions were flown against troop concentrations at Dolni Beneshov and Bela. The Il-2 Type 3s also hit the railway station at Smolkov on 16 April, but the formation ran into very heavy anti-aircraft defenses and more than twenty were damaged. Later that evening the unit attacked two bridges over the Oder river.

On 16 April 1945, during an attack on the Oder bridges, rear gunner Flight Sergeant Richard Husman, a former member of No 311 Squadron, Royal Air Force, shot down a Fw 190 near Olza; however, his Stormovik was damaged and barely made it home.

During these first days of operations no losses were recorded, but a number of Stormoviks sustained heavy damage, leaving twenty-three aircraft fully operational. On 19 April 1945 the unit flew seven missions against troop concentrations around Zabelkow, Kopytov and Novy Bohumin. During one such raid, the first Czech Il-2 (flown by Warrant Officer P. Slatinsky and Corporal J. Bilka) was reported as missing in action. On 20 April, the unit returned to Zabelkow, Kopytov and Novy Bohumin, in addition to flying two reconnaissance flights.

Il-2 Type 3s of the 421st Assault Aviation Regiment at Nis Air Force Base during early 1946. The Red Star on the White spinner of the second aircraft in the row, indicates that it was assigned to the Regiment's Commanding Officer. (Milan Micevski)

During one of these missions, the Il-2 Type 3 (Serial Number 12438, Red 38), flown by Flying Officer K. Novotny and rear gunner Sergeant L. Leng, was so badly damaged that the engine failed. The pilot crash landed between the front lines with armed bombs, that fortunately did not explode. During the advance of the Red Army, the Il-2 was discovered and the dismantled aircraft was returned to the Regiment. This Il-2 is now beautifully restored as part of the Aviation and Cosmonautics Museum at Prague-Kbely.

On 28 April the unit flew one of the most costly missions flown since the unit entered combat. During the morning the Regiment hit artillery batteries near the village of Ludgerovice. During an attack on Privoz, Red 02 was damaged. Flight Sergeant Jarolim Gucman's Il-2, Blue 30, was hit in the engine by German anti-aircraft fire over Wodzislaw. He made an emergency landing in an open field but was killed when the rear fuselage fuel tank exploded. Flight Sergeant Jarolim Gucman was the last Slovak pilot to die during the war. His rear gunner, Corporal Jan Valko, survived the crash with serious injuries. At the end of that day, the unit only had fifteen air worthy Il-2s. The soft muddy field prevented any further operations until 2 May 1945, when the unit's last mission was flown against the railway station of Tesin. Eight aircraft were dispatched and seven found the target.

During their brief operational career, the 3rd Czechoslovak Battle Regiment flew 284 sorties

During an attack against Privoz on 28 April 1945, Flight Sergeant Jarolim Gucman's Il-2 Type 3, Blue 30, of the 3rd Czechoslovak Battle Regiment was hit by German anti-aircraft fire over Wodzislaw. He managed to make an emergency landing in an open field, but was killed when the rear fuselage fuel tank exploded. His rear gunner, Corporal Jan Valko survived the crash, with serious injuries. (Zdenek Hurt)

A Czech Air Force Il-2 Type 3 (known as B-31s in Czech service) on the ramp at a Czech air base during the late 1940s. The aircraft was camouflaged with Dark Green uppersurfaces over Light Blue undersurfaces. (Zdenek Titz)

and destroyed one enemy fighter, forty-five trucks, twenty-two other vehicles, one locomotive, thirty-seven wagons and two fuel tanks. They also destroyed one ammunition stockpile, two munitions stocks, three buildings and sixty-eight anti-aircraft positions. Eight Il-2 Type 3s were lost during operations in the Ostrava area. Four were lost to enemy action while the other four were written off in non-combat accidents and crashes.

On 10 May 1945, the 3rd Czechoslovak Battle Regiment was transferred to Albrechticky near Pribor in Moravia. Between 14 and 22 May 1945 the unit was based at Prague-Kbely. On 20 July, the remaining twenty-five Il-2 Type 3s and the two Il-2UTs were officially transferred from the Red Air Force to the Czechoslovak Ministry of Defense and the unit was later renumbered the 30th Attack Regiment and based at Trencanske-Biskupice.

In Czech Air Force service the Il-2 Type 3 was designated B-31 and the Il-2UT became CB-31. In honor, to the area, the unit fought during the closing days of the Great Patriotic War, the 30th Attack Regiment received the honorary name *Ostrava*. The last B-31s and CB-31s were withdrawn from service during 1950.

Bulgaria

In 1941, Bulgaria, a largely agricultural country with a constitutional monarchy under Zsar Boris III, found itself allied with Nazi Germany. On 12 December 1942, Bulgaria declared war to the United States and England, but remained neutral in its dealing with the Soviet Union. On 8 September 1944, the Red Army invaded Bulgaria and a day later a Moscow supported government, under Minister Georgieff came to power, declaring war on Germany

In early 1945, a Soviet Technical Commission arrived in Bulgaria to modernize the Bulgarian Air Force, which was at that time, with the exception of the Messerschmitt Bf 109, a rather obsolete force.

On 14 March 1945, an agreement was signed to rebuild the Bulgarian Air Force under Soviet sponsorship. As part of the military assistance program, ninety-six Il-2 Type 3s and three Il-2UT trainers were delivered in April of 1945, these were followed later by an additional seven Il-2UTs. These aircraft were all based at Plovdiv airfield.

When the wooden fuselage of the Il-2s showed the first signs of corrosion they were replaced by all metal fuselages, built by the Zemunkiy Ikar factory in Yugoslavia. Some 100 all-metal fuselages were obtained in exchange for Bulgarian Air Force Messerschmitt Bf 109G-6s, which were turned over to the Yugoslavian Air Force as payment.

The Bulgarian Il-2 Type 3s were used mainly in the Assault Aviation Regiments, but a number were also used as flying observation posts for spotting artillery fire. The last example of the Il-2 Type 3 was phased out, along with the Il-10, in the Spring of 1958.

Il-2 Type 3M

During late 1941, Ilyushin started first work to re-arm the Il-2 with large caliber cannons. While the VYa-23 23MM cannon could penetrate enemy armor, its warhead was not large enough to inflict heavy damage to armored vehicles equipped with thick armor plate.

As part of the test program, a single seat Il-2 had its VYa-23 cannon replaced by a Sh-37 37MM cannon mounted in a gondola under each wing. The two wing mounted machine guns were retained. The gondola housed the gun and its ammunition supply (forty rounds) since it was technically impossible to install the heavy weapon and the ammunition supply in the wing itself as it was the case with the VYa-23.

The flying characteristics of the Il-2 with the under wing cannon suffered, due to a shift in the center of gravity. Firing tests also revealed that the gun had a strong recoil forces, which could damage the gondola mountings. As a result of these tests, this prototype was the only Il-2 fitted with the Sh-37 cannon.

In March of 1943, the NS-37 37MM cannon was installed in a production Il-2 Type 3 under the designation Il-2 Type 3M. The NS-37 had entered service during 1942. It weighed 330 pounds (150 kg) and had a rate of fire of 250 rounds per minute. The NS-37 could penetrate armor up to 48MM thick.

Like the earlier Sh-37, the NS-37 was housed in a under wing gondola together with its ammunition supply (50 rounds). Fully loaded, the gondola weighed 522 pounds (237 kg) and, as a measure to reduce the aircraft's overall weight, the four underwing rocket rails were deleted and the maximum bomb load, which could be carried in the underwing bomb bays, was reduced to 440 pounds (200 kg). The VYa-23 cannons were deleted, while the 7.62MM machine guns were retained for aiming purposes. The tail wheel was four inches (10 cm) higher and the tail wheel fairing was also enlarged.

Flight tests, which lasted between late March and April of 1943, revealed that, when the aircraft was fully armed, the center of gravity had shifted by 3.5 percent to the rear. As a result, the Il-2 Type 3M required considerably piloting skill and had much more demanding flight characteristics.

Firing trials with the Il-2 Type 3M revealed that the recoil of the NS-37 cannon damaged the gondola mountings and, as a result, recoil dampers were incorporated in the gondola.

The Il-2 Type 3M went into action during the battle of Kursk in July of 1943, where the Germans had assembled some 2,700 tanks and self-propelled guns for Operation CITADEL, the German summer offensive against the Red Army. The NS-37 quickly proved that it could knock out Panther and Tiger tanks on the Kursk battlefield.

The Il-2 Type 3M prototype was armed with a Sh-37 37MM cannon mounted in an underwing gondola. The gondola housed the gun and forty rounds of ammunition. (G. F. Petrov)

Ground crews remove the tree branches used as camouflage from a IL-2 Type 3M. The underwing gondola on the production variant had a more slanted front and housed a NS-37 cannon in place of the Sh-37 used on the prototype. Additionally, the aircraft had a slightly taller tail wheel strut and the underwing rocket rails were deleted. (G.F. Petrov)

The Il-2 Type 3 and the Il-2 Type 3M made a significant contribution to the Soviet victory at Kursk, flying countless sorties against German troops and tanks. Il-2s destroyed seventy tanks in twenty minutes on 7 July 1943. In a four-hour assault on the 17th Panzer Division, Il-2s destroyed 240 tanks out of an approximate strength of 300. At the end of the battle in August of 1943, the Wehrmacht had lost 500,000 men, 1,500 tanks and over 3,700 aircraft. The Il-2 Type 3M was also used by the Soviet Naval Aviation for anti-shipping missions.

The number of Il-2 Type 3Ms remained, when compared to the Il-2 Type 3, rather limited. One of the reasons for the low production numbers, besides the demanding flight characteristics, was a shortage of NS-37 weapons. The Il-2 Type 3M was used exclusively by the Soviet Air Force and was not exported.

In early 1945, a Il-2 Type 3M was rearmed with two NS-45 45MM cannon in place of the standard NS-37s. Althought the tests were successful, the war ended and the project was cancelled.

NS-37 Cannon Gondola

Sh-37 Cannon   **NS-37 Cannon**

Il-2UT Trainer

In 1943 the first two seat trainer variant of the Il-2, the Il-2UT, entered production. Prior to this time, pilots had received their conversion training on the Sukhoi Su-2 bomber, which had the same take-off and landing speeds as the Il-2. The Su-2 had very bad flying characteristics and a 1,330 hp M-82 radial engine. In short, the Su-2 was far from being ideally suited for training Il-2 pilots. Other Il-2 pilots were first checked out in the Li-2 transport before they made their first Il-2 solo flight. In the fast paced training program in the Assault Aviation Training Centers, pilots seldom had more as ten hours of Il-2 flight time before they were sent to the front. These pilots had very rudimentary flying skills, and lacked proper training in navigation and combat tactics. Only a few of these "green pilots" were aware that the Il-2 was nearly as nimble as an enemy fighter. With training in evasive action, the lives of many inexperienced pilots could have been saved.

The Il-2UT replaced the rear gunner's compartment with a second dual control cockpit for the instructor. Additionally, the fuselage tank was reduced in size to gain space for the instrument panel and the second cockpit. The instructor's cockpit had a rear sliding canopy and a solid fairing was installed behind the instructor's seat. The antenna mast was relocated to the front canopy framing.

In order to save weight, the two wing mounted VYa-23 cannons were deleted and some Il-2UTs had two instead of four underwing rocket rails (many Il-2UTs had no rocket rails). For weapons training, the two 7.62MM machine guns were retained along with an ammunition supply of 1,500 rounds per gun and the bomb bays could be loaded with up to 1,700 pounds of bombs. Some Il-2UT had these guns deleted and were only used for advanced training.

A number of canopy versions were produced on the Il-2UT during its production life. Most

A Il-2UT during an inspection. This trainer had a single Type RO rocket rail fitted under the wing for armament training. The aircraft had side armor panels on the rear instructor's canopy. The Il-2UT had the radio antenna mast relocated from the rear canopy framing to the forward canopy framing. (G.F. Petrov)

Fuselage Development

Il-2 Type 3

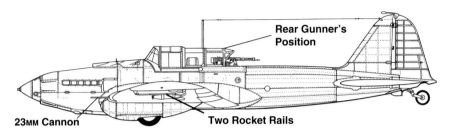

Rear Gunner's Position

23MM Cannon   Two Rocket Rails

Il-2UT

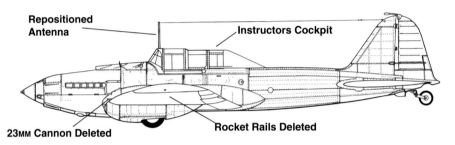

Repositioned Antenna   Instructors Cockpit

23MM Cannon Deleted   Rocket Rails Deleted

of the wartime Il-2UTs had side armor plate fitted on the instructor's canopy. Other wartime Il-2UTs also had armor on top of the instructors canopy. In order to provide the pupil with a better view to the side, some Il-2UT had the side armor plate replaced by a large side glazed panel. Postwar Il-2UTs generally deleted all the armor plates in favor of glazed panels.

This rather weathered Il-2UT was assigned to the Naval Aviation Regiment of the Northern Fleet. Both canopies have had the side armor removed and replaced with glazed panel. A instruction is giving the next class of students their introduction to the aircraft during 1948. (G.F. Petrov)

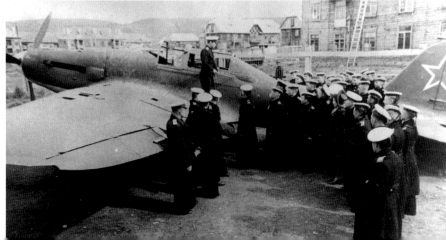

A limited number of Il-2UTs were produced on the same production line as the Il-2 Type 3 until production was terminated during 1945. They were mainly used at the Assault Aviation Training Centers, although a few were allocated to combat units, usually a single Il-2UT being assigned to each Assault Aviation Regiment.

A number of Il-2UT were also modified as target tugs for anti-aircraft units, towing a target on a wire in safe distance behind the trainer.

Exports

Poland had a total of twelve Il-2UTs on strength in late December of 1944. On 1 May 1945, with the exception of the 3rd Assault Aviation Regiment, each regiment was assigned a single Il-2UT with a total of fifteen being assigned to the Polish Air Force. On 1 September 1949, a total of thirty-two Il-2UTs were in the inventory to the Polish Air Force, assigned to the 4th Assault Aviation Regiment (six), the 5th Assault Aviation Regiment (five) and the 6th Assault Aviation Regiment (seven), as well on a single Naval Aviation Regiment. Thirteen were assigned to the Officers Aviation School.

The Yugoslav Assault Aviation Training Center at Zemun Air Base near Belgrade had three Il-2UTs during the war. Due to a shortage of trainers for the six Assault Aviation Regiments in the Yugoslav Air Force, the Zemunkiy Ikar factory converted about twenty-five Il-2 Type 3s to Il-2UT trainer standard.

The 3rd Czechoslovak Battle Regiment had two Il-2UTs. In Czech Air Force service the Il-2UT was designated CB-31. The 3rd Czechoslovak Battle Regiment was later renumbered the 30th Attack Regiment and was based at Trencanske-Biskupice. One Il-2UT was unarmed and remained in service until the Summer of 1948. The other Il-2UT was damaged during a

A line-up of the 3rd Czechoslovak Battle Regiment's Il-2 Type 3 and Lavochkin La-5FN fighters at Prague-Kbely airfield when the unit was formally handed over from the Red Air Force to the newly formed Czech Air Force. The aircraft in the foreground was one the two Il-2UTs assigned to the regiment. The aircraft retained a ShKAS 7.62MM machine gun in the wing for gunnery training. (Zdenek Hurt)

crash landing on 18 August 1948. After repairs it rejoined the 30th Attack Regiment. In early 1951 the aircraft crashed again and was then struck off charge.

Bulgaria received, as part of the Soviet modernization program for the Bulgarian Air Force, three Il-2UTs during April of 1945. Later, an additional seven Il-2UTs were delivered. A number of Il-2 Type 3s were also converted to trainer standards by the Bulgarian Air Force. These aircraft were all based at Plovdiv airfield and were struck of charge during late 1953.

One of thirty-two Il-2UTs which were used by the Polish Air Force. The tactical number on this overall Dark Green trainer was carried in large White digits on the fuselage. (Andrzej Morgala)

This Il-2UT, Red 8, belongs to the Yugoslav Assault AviationTraining Center at Zemun Air Base near Belgrade. The side armor on the pilot's canopy has been replaced by a large glazed panel. (Milan Micevski)

Il-10

During the Autumn of 1943 the Ilyushin OKB began development of a replacement for the Il-2 Type 3 in the assault role. The new aircraft would have improved armor protection, especially for the rear gunner, and the flight characteristics and maneuverability were to be such that the aircraft would be able to outmaneuver current German fighters.

Combat reports from Assault Aviation Regiment crews were carefully analyzed in order to improve the general shortcomings of the Il-2 Type 3. The new design was to be powered by the 2,000 hp AM-42 power plant being developed by the Mikulin Design Bureau.

The new assault aircraft project was the result of close cooperation between the Ilyushin OKB, the Central Aero and Hydrodynamics Institute and the examination of countless combat reports. Combat experience had shown that the armor thickness around the lower engine should be extended, while on the other hand, the armor protection for the upper part of the power plant could be reduced since this area was less likely to be hit by ground fire.

The armored cockpit shell was extended to include the rear gunner. In the Il-2 Type 3, the pilot and gunner were separated by the main fuselage fuel tank, but in the new aircraft, the crew was seated back to back, separated by a back armor plate. The main fuel tank (116 gallons, 440 liters) was repositioned between the engine and the cockpit. A second tank (77 gallons, 290 liters) was located under the pilot's cockpit.

The side armor protection of the pilot and the rear gunner included two parallel fixed 8MM amour plates with the space between the plates filled with air. This new armor layout would protect the pilot and the gunner from ground fire up to 20MM.

The pilot's seat had no fore and aft adjustment, but could be raised or lowered (on the ground). In the rear cockpit, the gunner was seated on a small ledge that protruded from the

Fuselage Development

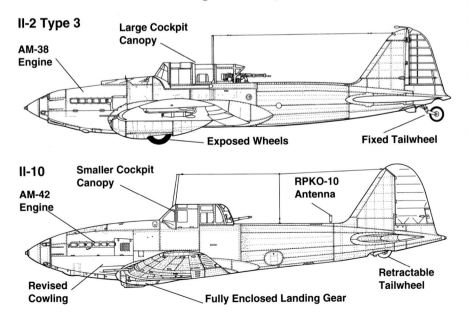

Il-2 Type 3

- AM-38 Engine
- Large Cockpit Canopy
- Exposed Wheels
- Fixed Tailwheel

Il-10

- AM-42 Engine
- Smaller Cockpit Canopy
- RPKO-10 Antenna
- Revised Cowling
- Fully Enclosed Landing Gear
- Retractable Tailwheel

This Il-I0 of the 571st Assault Aviation Regiment made a belly landing during a mission over occupied East Germany on 15 April 1945. The bent propeller blades indicate that the AM-42 engine was running at when the aircraft touched down. (Ivan Ivanov)

armor plate and separated the front and rear cockpits. There was a web sling provided to support the gunner when he was standing to operate the turret.

Research data supplied by the Central Aero and Hydrodynamics Institute resulted in a much cleaner design and wind tunnel testing revealed that it had fifty per cent less aerodynamic drag than the Il-2 Type 3.

A total of three prototypes were assembled at GAZ-18. During February of 1944, the first prototype was finished; however, there was no power plant available. While awaiting the power plant, the aircraft was dismantled and shipped, on 15 February 1944, to Zhukovsky. There it was assembled and mated with an AM-42 engine. The type, now designated the Il-10, made its first flight on 18 April 1944 with test pilot V. K. Kokkinaki at the controls.

The Il-10 differed from the Il-2 in a number of ways. The wingspan was reduced from 48 feet (14.6 meters) to 44 feet (13.4 meters) and the fuselage length was reduced from 38 feet (11.65 meters) to 36.5 feet 1(11.12 meters). These changes improve the aircraft's maneuverability and flight characteristics.

The offensive armament of the Il-10 was the same as the Il-2 Type 3, two VYa-23 cannons with 150 rounds per gun and two ShKAS 7.62MM machine guns with 750 rounds per gun.

On 13 May 1944, the Il-10 was transferred to the Flight Research Institute at Zhukovsky for the State Acceptance Trials, which only lasted two weeks. The evaluation revealed that the Il-10, with a take off weight of 13,966 pounds (6,335 kg), had a top speed of 342 mph (551 km/h), at 9,186 feet (2,800 meters), 93 mph (150 km/h) faster than the a Il-2 Type 3. At altitudes between ground level and 6,500 feet (2,000 meters) the Il-10 was only six mph (10 km/h) to nine mph (15 km/h) slower than the Bf-109G-2 and Fw-190A-4.

The State Acceptance Trials and weapons evaluation by the Scientific Research Institute of the Red Air Force were so enthusiastic that the People's Commissariat for Armament cleared the type for production in August of 1944. The first production Il-10 left the assembly lines at GAZ-18 in October of 1944. Initially the type had a low production rate, in order not to interfere with the output of Il-2 Type 3s.

The production Il-10 differed from the Il-2 Type 3 in a number of ways. The use of the AM-42 engine resulted in a number of changes to the nose of the Il-10. The small air intake under the nose on the Il-2 was deleted on the Il-10, as was the radiator intake on top of the nose. All Il-2s had five large and one small exhaust stacks. The Il-10 has six large exhaust stacks. The bulged fairing behind the exhaust on the Il-2 was replaced by a flat panel with five vents. While the AM-38F drove an AV-5L-158 propeller, the Il-10 was equipped with an

A line-up of Il-I0s on an airfield in the Eastern Zone of Occupied Germany during the late 1940s. These aircraft carried their tactical markings in White at the base of the vertical fin. All are equipped with a direction finder antenna on the fuselage spine in front of the fin. (Carl-Fredrik Geust)

This Hungarian Air Force Il-10, Yellow 33, had a landing gear failure on landing at Tapolca. The Yellow wing insignia on the fin was carried by all Tapolca based Il-10s and was introduced in May of 1953. The aircraft also had an Orange spinners. (George Punka)

propeller. The large sand-filter installed in the starboard wing root of the Il-2M and Il-2 Type 3 was relocated under the wing center section on the Il-10.

The offensive armament of the production Il-10 remained the same as the prototypes, although a S-13 gun camera was added in a fairing on the starboard wing. The cannon barrel fairing of the VYa-23 cannon was modified with an additional blister above the barrel on the Il-10. The rear armament consisted of a UBK 12.7MM gun with 150 rounds mounted in a VU-8 turret. The VU-8 turret had a field of fire of 50 degrees elevation, 18 degrees depression and 45 degrees in azimuth.

While the Il-2 Type 3 was equipped with four bomb bays in the wing, the Il-10 had only two bays, located just inboard of the landing gear wheel well. The Il-10 also had two externally Type D3-42 bomb racks for bombs up to 551 pounds (250 kg). The Il-2 Type 3 was equipped with four rocket rails, Il-10s produced during the war deleted the rails, although there were provisions for mounting the rails within the wings; however, due to their poor accuracy, rockets were usually not used on Il-10s.

The main undercarriage members pivoted on the forward spar of the two-spar wing to turn through 90 degrees and lie flat in the wing. The main wheel fairings and the main undercarriage doors were also considerably reduced in size.

The landing gear, wing flaps, brakes and starter, were all pneumatic and there were two low-pressure air cylinders for normal operations and one high pressure cylinder for emergency operations. When the AM-42 engine was running, a Type AK-50 direct-drive air compressor maintained pressure in the system. Late production Il-10s had a AK-75 compressor.

The access hatches for the armament were changed in layout in order to obtain easier maintenance and rearming in the field. While the Il-2 Type 3 had rounded wing tips, the Il-10 had blunter wing tips. The position light on each wingtip was repositioned to the inner rear of the wing.

There were two air intakes in the wing roots of the Il-10, these fed air to the oil coolers and fed induction air to the AM-42 engine. The air passed through the supercharger into the central induction pipe and then to the carburetors.

The VV-1 gun sight of the Il-2 Type 3 was replaced by an PBP-lB gun sight fitted in the cockpit. The vertical radio mast on the rear canopy frame of the Il-2 Type 3 was replaced by a mast that was slightly slanted to the rear and mounted on the front canopy frame.

The rudder mass balance weight seen on all Il-2 variants was deleted on the Il-10, as was the rudder trim tab actuating rod. The Il-10 had a retractable, non-steerable tail wheel, and also had an AFA-1M camera in the rear fuselage underside.

The first Il-10s were assigned to the 108th Guards Assault Aviation Regiment (the former 299th Assault Aviation Regiment) in October of 1944 for conversion training. On 2 February 1945, the Il-10 entered combat with the 108th Guards Assault Aviation Regiment of the 2nd Air Army under the command of F.A. Shigarin . They attacked enemy tanks and infantry formations near Sprottau on the Neisse River.

Most Il-10s were allocated to Assault Aviation Regiments of the 2nd and 16th Air Army, which were engaged in the capture of Berlin and the liberation of Czechoslovakia. When the Great Patriotic War ended on 9 May 1945, some 466 Il-10 had been built, but only about one hundred of them had entered service. After the war, the Il-10 quickly replaced the Il-2 Type 3s in Assault Aviation Regiments based in the Soviet occupied zone of the former Third Reich.

While the Il-10 only saw limited combat in the war against Germany, it saw considerable action during the brief war with Japan. The Soviet Union, which remained neutral in the Pacific war, finally declared war on Japan on 8 August 1945, two days after the first atomic bomb. The Red Army under the command of Marshal A. M. Vasilvesky attacked Manchuria and on 12 August 1945, Soviet Forces landed in Korea.

The 253rd Assault Aviation Division, of the 10th Air Army, equipped with Il-10s, devoted most of its resources to the Soviet 25th Army and the Red Banner Amur River Flotilla. The 248th Assault Aviation Division of the 12th Air Army provided air support for advancing Soviet troops in Manchuria.

The Il-10 engaging Japanese vessels using a skip bombing tactic, similar to that used by American B-25s of the 5th Air Force. On 10 August 1945, six Il-10s, commanded by Captain I.F. Voronin attacked Japanese vessels in the harbor of Rasin. By using skip bombing, one vessel was sunk. In addition, a Japanese fighter attacking Voronin's Il-10 was shot down by the rear gunner.

Its improved armor protection and increased low-altitude agility combined to reduce the Il-10's vulnerability to ground fire, while its higher speeds and enhanced maneuverability increased its ability to evade fighter attack. It was easier to rearm and maintain in the field and its handling characteristics were immeasurably superior to its predecessor.

During the Great Patriotic War, the Il-10 was produced at GAZ-18, but in 1946 the State Aircraft Factory 71 at Voronezh, which had built Il-2s, started to build the Il-10 as well.

With the end of the war, production of the Il-10 continued with the aim to progressively

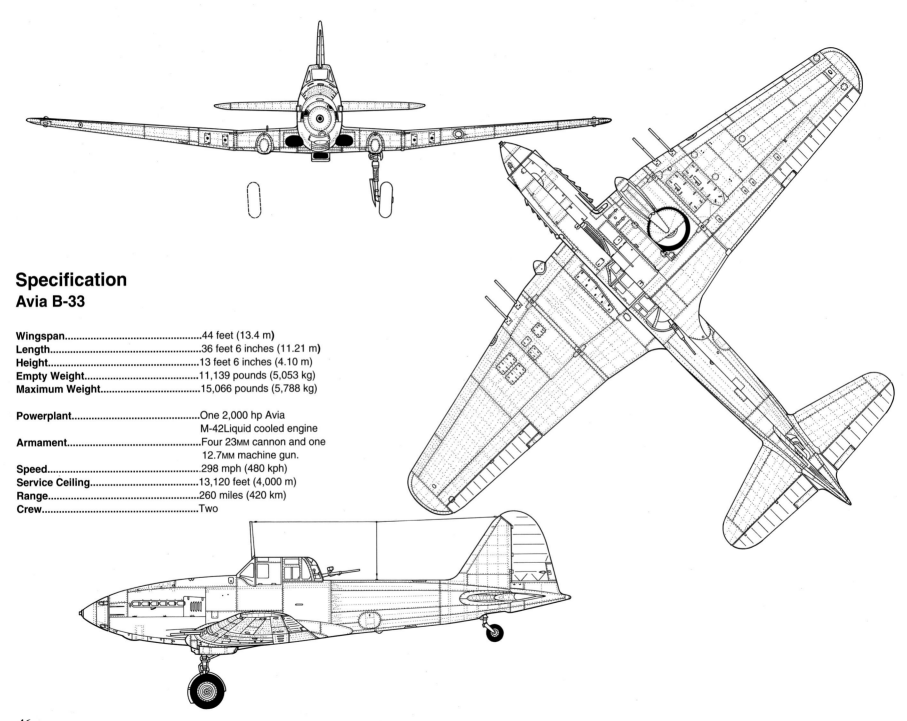

Specification
Avia B-33

Wingspan	44 feet (13.4 m)
Length	36 feet 6 inches (11.21 m)
Height	13 feet 6 inches (4.10 m)
Empty Weight	11,139 pounds (5,053 kg)
Maximum Weight	15,066 pounds (5,788 kg)
Powerplant	One 2,000 hp Avia M-42 Liquid cooled engine
Armament	Four 23мм cannon and one 12.7мм machine gun.
Speed	298 mph (480 kph)
Service Ceiling	13,120 feet (4,000 m)
Range	260 miles (420 km)
Crew	Two

A pair Szekesfehervar-Tac based Il-10 Parduc (Panther) armed with FAB-100 bombs on their external bomb racks. The Red arrow on the fin had a thin White outline. The aircraft in the foreground had a Light Blue spinner while the aircraft in the background had an Olive-Green spinner. (George Punka)

replace the Il-2 Type 3 in all Assault Aviation Regiments. For almost a decade, the Il-10 remained the backbone for the Assault Aviation Regiments in the Soviet Air Force before it was decided to replace these regiments with fighter-bomber units equipped with MiG-15s. The lessons learned, during the Korean conflict, made it obvious that the piston engined Il-10 would suffer very high losses to enemy jet fighters. In addition, the MiG-15 or Yak-23 fighters could not provide adequate escort protection, since they were simply to fast.

During operation with Soviet and Warsaw Pact Assault Aviation Regiments, the main wheel covers were often removed to prevent them from being damaged when the Il-10 had to operate from unprepared fields or soft ground.

When the RPKO-10M radio compass became available in the post-war period, Il-10s were fitted with this device. Externally Il-10s, with this feature, could be distinguished by the direction finder loop antenna mounted on the rear fuselage at the base of the rudder. This was the most common post-war variant of the Il-10 and many were exported outside of the Soviet Union.

Some late production Il-10s, built after the war, had the VU-8 turret replaced by a VU-9M turret armed with a BTN-20E 20MM cannon with 150 rounds. On late production Il-10s the standard armament of two 7.62MM machine guns and two 23MM cannons was replaced by two NS-23 23MM cannons with 150 rounds per gun. These lacked the barrel fairing seen on the VYa-23 cannon. The S-13 gun camera was relocated to a position on the starboard wing. Only a few of these NS-23 equipped Il-10 actually entered service with the Soviet Air Force and none of the NS-23 cannon equipped Il-10s were ever exported, although this late version was produced under license in Czechoslovakia.

The last Il-10 left the assembly lines at GAZ-18 during 1947, while the State Aircraft Factory 71 at Voronezh continued to produce the type until 1949. The Il-10 remained in service in with the Soviet Air Force and other friendly air forces when NATO introduced the ASCC Reporting Name System during mid-1955, and, as a result, the aircraft received the NATO code name Beast.

Il-10UT

Shortly before the end of the Great Patriotic War, the first prototype of the Il-l0UT two seat trainer was completed. The aircraft retained the same overall size of the fuselage, but a stretched rear sliding canopy was introduced for the rear instructor's cockpit which was outfitted with full dual controls. A glazed canopy section was installed between the front and the rear cockpits. The armor plate, separating the pilot's and rear cockpit,was deleted as was the headrests for both crew members.

The Il-10UT was armed with two 23MM cannons and two 7.62MM guns. But the trainers had no external bomb racks. Avionics and instrumentation was the same as the standard Il-10.

The first trainers were built at GAZ-18 in Kuibyshev but in 1946, GAZ-71, at Voronezh. also began building Il-10UTs. In 1949, production was phased out with a total of 100 Il-10UTs being built at Voronezh.

Since there was a chronic shortage of trainers within the Soviet Assault Aviation Regiments a number of single seat Il-10s were also converted to the two-seat trainer configuration at Field Maintenance Depots. Czechoslovakia and Hungary also converted a number of Il-10s to the trainer role.

Il-10M

In the late 1940s the Ilyushin launched a redesign and improvement program for the Il-10, even though it was obvious that the era of the piston engined heavy assault aircraft was over. The first Il-10M prototype was converted from a standard production Il-10 and had a two and a half foot (750MM) stretch added to the fuselage and the retractable tail wheel was moved more to the rear. The direction finding loop antenna was replaced by a fairing under the fuselage. A new wing with a Clark YH profile, that featured constant dihedral from the root, was fitted. This wing had the main landing gear leg knuckles enlarged and moved slightly outboard, increasing the wheel track by 10 per cent. The main wheels were enlarged and there were slight increases in fuel and oil capacities.

The four NS-23 23MM cannons, fitted on the last production batches of the Il-10, were replaced by NR-23 23MM cannons with an ammunition supply of 150 rounds per gun. The NR-23 had an improved ammunition feed system and a higher rate of fire, 850 rounds per minute instead of 550 rpm. The empty weight rose from 4,650 kg (Il-10) to the 5,570 kg (Il-10M) and the gross weight went from 6,500 kg to 7,320 kg.

The Il-10M prototype flew for the first time in the Summer of 1951 with Vladimir K. Kokinaki at the controls. The performance of the Il-10M was generally inferior to that of the Il-10. The top speed dropped from 551 km/h on the Il-10 to 476 km/h on the Il-10M prototype.

The Il-10M prototype was fitted with an entirely new wing with NR-23 cannons in place of the NS-23KM guns. The aircraft also had a wiper blade added to the windscreen. The Il-10M was built in small numbers and saw only limited service. (Ivan Ivanov)

A pair of Czech Air Force Avia B-33s. In contrast to the usual Warsaw Pact practice of no upper wing markings, Czech B-33s carried the national insignia on the wing uppersurfaces. The tactical codes on the fuselage were White. (Zdenek Titz)

type. The rate of climb was also reduced, the Il-10 needed 1.6 minutes to climb to 1,000 meters, the Il-10M needed 2.1 minutes.

The Il-10M was built in small numbers between 1951 and 1954, but the performance of the Il-10 during the early stages of the Korean conflict clearly showed that the aircraft would suffer heavy losses on the modern battlefield. Between 1944 and 1954 a total of 4,966 Il-10s and Il-10Ms had been built in the Soviet Union.

Avia B-33

In the late 1940s, negotiations were started to produce the Il-10 under license in Czechoslovakia for export to countries within the Soviet sphere of influence. This decision was taken to allow the Soviet Union to concentrate their resources to the manufacture of more sophisticated aircraft such as the MiG-15 fighter and Il-28 twin engined jet medium bomber.

The production of the Il-10 was phased out at Voronezh during 1949 and a short time later all documentation on the type was transferred to Czechoslovakia. It was planned to produce the aircraft in the Avia plant at Cakovice near the Czech capital of Prague. An early production Soviet built Il-10 served as a pattern aircraft, although the variant to be produced would be the late production aircraft equipped with four NS-23 23MM cannons. Additionally, VU-8 turret was replaced by an BTN-20E 20MM cannon in the VU-9M turret.

The first B-33 (Serial 1073) assembled at the Avia plant, made its first flight on 26 December 1951. This aircraft was powered by a Soviet-built AM-38 engine since the Czech license built Avia M-42 power plant had not been certified for production. On 13 May 1952 the second prototype B-33 (Serial 1074) successfully passed its first factory test flight. This aircraft was equipped with a Czech manufactured M-42 power plant and served as a pattern aircraft for the production version.

The two external differences between a late production Il-10s and the Czech B-33s were the lack of a direction finding loop antenna on the rear fuselage and, while all Soviet built Il-10s had a slightly backward slanted radio mast, the B-33s had a vertical radio mast. In addition, there was no provision for a DAG-10 dispenser on Czech built B-33s. Early B-33 had a S-13 gun camera fitted in the starboard wing, but most B-33s had the gun camera deleted and the opening faired over.

The B-33s experienced some teething problems which were overcome through a joint modernization and improvement program by the Avia plant and the Flight Research Institute. When these problems were all solved, large scale production started at Cakovice during late 1952. With the exception of the BTN-20E cannon, which was imported from the Soviet Union, most parts for the B-33 were produced in Czechoslovakia.

Fuselage Development

B-33

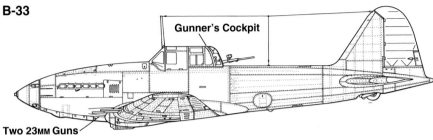

Gunner's Cockpit

Two 23MM Guns

CB-33

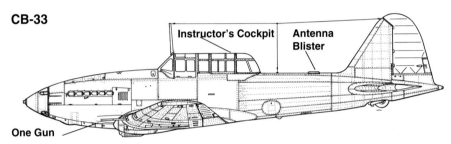

Instructor's Cockpit   Antenna Blister

One Gun

Late Avia B-33s differed from the standard production planes in having a triangle shaped, slightly forward slanted radio mast. On a number of these aircraft, a non-retractable tail wheel was introduced. Late production B-33s were also fitted with a short barreled version of the BTN-20E cannon. Some late production B-33 were also equipped with the AFP-21 camera for photographic missions at low altitude. The AFP-21 replaced the original AFA-IM camera fitted on the Soviet built Il-10 and most Czech-built B-33s. For night missions, an AFP-21N or an AFP-21 infrared camera could be carried in place of the day camera.

The last Avia B-33 left the assembly line during 1955. Although these aircraft were considered obsolete, the production line was not closed earlier, simply to fulfill the goals of the Five Year Plan. Since other countries refused to accept further deliveries of the B-33, many factory fresh B-33 were stored on airfields in Czechoslovakia for three years before they were scrapped.

B-33s in the Czech Air Force were progressively updated. An avionics fairing was installed on the rear upper fuselage centerline and two revised T-shaped antennas for a RV-2 radio.

This Czech CB-33 trainer was assigned to the Flight Research Institute and carries the Institute fuselage code, V-10 in White. This CB-33 carried no armament, but others usually were armed with a single 23MM cannon in each wing. (Zdenek Titz)

altimeter were fitted on the lower fuselage. In the mid-1950s, the JRRO-130 tube launched, unguided rocket was introduced and some B-33s were outfitted to use this weapon. Other B-33s were equipped with a net under the wing to collect the shells during firing trials. All these features were unique to Czech Air Force B-33s.

In 1958 the Assault Aviation Division was disbanded, but some regiments continued to operate B-33s in the reconnaissance and observation roles. The type was also well suited to the forward air controller role, directing artillery fire. A number of B-33s and CB-33 trainers served the Flight Research Institute as test-beds for various items of equipment, including Czech manufactured parachutes and armament. A B-33 served as a test bed for the evaluation for the rail launched LR-130 unguided rocket and this same aircraft conducted tests with German SC-70 bombs. The last flight of a B-33 was on 26 April 1962.

CB-33

During 1952, the Czech Avia factory at Cakovice began producing a trainer variant of the B-33 designated the CB-33. The CB-33 was delivered both as an armed and unarmed trainer versions. Some of the armed variants carried the same cannon armament as the B-33, four NS-23KM 23MM cannon, while most were armed with two NS-23KM cannons. CB-33s, intended as pure trainers, were delivered with no armament and the slots for the shell ejectors on the under side of the wing were faired over. Late Avia built CB-33s differed from the standard production trainers in having a triangle shaped, slightly forward slanted radio mast. These late production CB-33s had the rear sliding rear canopy replaced by a canopy which opened to the starboard side. Production of the CB-33 was phased out during 1955.

Exports

A number of early and standard production Il-10 were exported to countries within Moscow's sphere of influence. Most were not factory fresh, but were transferred from Soviet Assault Aviation Regiments, when they converted to the late production Il-10 with four NS-23 cannons. All were equipped with the direction finder loop antenna on the rear fuselage, just in front of the tail. Czech built B-33 were never directly exported from the Avia factory to a

A line-up of Avia B-33s assigned to the Polish 30th Naval Aviation Regiment. These aircraft were modified with underwing rocket rails. The fairing on the centerline of the lower fuselage housed an ADF antenna. The straight antenna mast was another identification feature for the B-33. (Mariusz Konarski)

American Marines look over a burned out North Korean Air Force Il-10, Yellow 39, destroyed on the ground by United Nations aircraft at Kimpo Air Field. (Larry Davis)

client country. The export of B-33s was handled by the Ministry of Defense and the Czech Air Force. The aircraft were delivered to the Czech Air Force and then flown to military airfields. Czech Air Force pilots then ferried the aircraft to the destination country, where they were handled over. B-33s were exported to Bulgaria, Poland, Romania and North Yemen.

The People's Republic of Bulgaria received its first Soviet built Il-10 in 1948 to equip a single Assault Aviation Regiment, which was based at Plovdiv Air Base. Later, the country took delivery of a number of Czech manufactured B-33s. They were phased out in the Spring of 1958.

The Czechs received their first Soviet-built Il-10s in late Summer of 1950. These aircraft were allocated to the 30th Assault Aviation Regiment of the 4th Mixed Aviation Division. When sufficient numbers of B-33s from Czech production became available, the original Soviet Il-10s were quickly withdrawn from service.

Hungary received its first fifty Il-10s between 9 and 14 September 1949. Another nine were delivered in November of 1950 and between the 17 February 1953 and 7 July 1953, another 100 Il-10s arrived.

These were all ex-Soviet Air Force aircraft and some showed signs of battle damage and it was generally assumed by the Hungarians that these had once served in Korea. During general overhaul in Hungary, it was also found that some of these Il-10 had no less then three different layers of paint. A total of 159 Soviet built Il-10s were used in Hungary and according to Hungarian tradition, the type received the name *Parduc* (Panther).

The first Il-10s were allocated to an Assault Aviation Squadron of the Mixed Regiment based at Kecskemet and to the Aviation Officers Academy at Szolnok. Between 1949 and 1951, Hungarian national markings were very similar to those of the North Korean Air Force. The Red star on the White background was surrounded by three circles. The inner circle was Green, followed by a White and a Red circle. This style of national markings was changed in

This partially dismantled Il-10, Yellow 44, awaits shipment to the United States alongside a second North Korean Air Force Il-10, Yellow 55. Both aircraft have had their rear armament removed and their canopies protected by a canvas covering. (USAF)

1951 in favor of a Red star with a White circle and a Red dot in the center. On 1 October 1951, three Assault Aviation Regiments were formed and each regiment could be identified by the color of the aircraft's spinner: Orange for Tapolca, Lemon-Yellow Borgond and Light-Blue for Szekesfehervar-Tac. During 1955, the Supreme Command of the Hungarian Air Force replaced the piston engined Il-10s with by MiG-15s. As a result the remaining Il-10 and Il-10UT were scrapped.

The Republic of Indonesia obtained a number of ex-Polish B-33s during 1957. The negotiations for these aircraft were carried out under very strict security. The B-33 destined for Indonesia were converted for long range duties and two wet points were fitted in the mid-wing area in order to accommodate two 400 liter underwing fuel tanks. The Indonesians were not pleased with the B-33 and, as a result, all were re-crated, returned to Poland and scrapped.

The Democratic People's Republic of Korea (North Korea) received a number of Soviet built Il-10 before the outbreak of the Korean War. On 25 June 1950, a massive surprise attack was launched against the Republic of Korea and a number of low level attacks were performed by North Korean Assault Aviation Regiments during the opening phase of the Korean conflict. Some of the Il-10s attacked Seoul and its Kimpo airport, causing panic among the civilians. A number of attacks were also made against South Korean troops. But generally, the contribution of the Il-10 during the initial stage of the conflict was very slight.

On 27 June 1950, eight Il-10s from Yonpo Air Base crossed Seoul heading for Kimpo airfield were intent on disrupting the refugee airlift. Before they could commence their attack, they were bounced by four F-80s of the 35th FBS and within minutes the four surviving Il-10s were heading for the sanctuary of their own territory. After this engagement, the North Koreans refrained from sending more aircraft to the Seoul-Kimpo area.

During the initial stage of the Korean conflict the United Nation forces captured at least three intact Il-10 at various airfields. A number of damaged Il-10 also felt into United Nation forces hands during their advance into the North. Two Il-10s, bearing the tactical numbers, Yellow 44 and Yellow 55, were found by USAF personnel in the demolished hangars of Kimpo airfield when United Nations troops seized the field in September of 1950.

These Il-10s found were subsequently shipped, still carrying full North Korean markings to the Wright Air Development Center at Wright Petterson AFB, Dayton, Ohio. Before flight testing began, the North Korean markings were replaced by American national markings. The North Korean tactical numbers remained on the tail along with a Wright Air Development

Yellow 44 was test flown at the Wright Air Development Center, Wright Patterson AFB, Ohio carrying the ADC registration T2-3000 on the tail and USAF markings on the rear fuselage during the Summer of 1951. A total of eleven flights were conducted with the Il-10. (USAF)

Many CB-33s ended their days as test beds. This Czech CB-33, White 6, was used as an armament test bed and was equipped with cannons and underwing missile launch rails. (Zdenek Hurt)

Center registration number.

The test program lasted from 20 June 1951 to 15 August 1951 and consisted of eleven flights totaling 13 hours and 55 minutes, which were flown by Captain R.L. Stephens of the Flight Test Division. The tests were conducted to aid the Air Technical Intelligence Center in making future estimates of the performance of foreign aircraft. Captain Stephens reported that, as a result of the counterclockwise rotation of the propeller, the aircraft had a tendency to pull to the right, in sharp contrast to USAF single-engine aircraft, which had a tendency to pull to the left.

Poland received its first Soviet manufactured Il-10 during 1949. Initially Poland refused deliveries of the Il-10 because the type was regarded as obsolete. A total of forty Il-10s were assigned to the three Assault Aviation Wings, which were at that time also equipped with the Il-2 Type 3 and as a result, mixed formations with both types were formed.

In early 1953s about fifty Czech-built B-33 arrived and were assigned to the 30th Navy Aviation Wing. Polish pilots were not impressed by the Il-10 and B-33. During operation, the AM-42 engines would often seize and this led to a number of crashes and forced landing. From mid-1957 onward, the Polish Air Force started to progressively withdraw all remaining Il-10s and B-33s from service. The last Il-10 and B-33 were retired from Polish Air Force service during late 1959 and scrapped.

In March of 1953, the first thirty Soviet built Il-10s and Il-10UTs were delivered to Romania to equip the three Regiments of the 68th Assault Aviation Group. Most of the aircraft received were ex-Soviet Air Force and showed signs of extreme wear. In April of 1953, a total of 150 Czech built B-33 and CB-33 were delivered and, as a result of this shipment, Romania became the largest operator of the B-33 outside of Czechoslovakia. Each of the three Regiments received forty-five aircraft and fifteen were sent to the Aurel Vlaicu Aviation School at Bobocu. With the delivery of the B-33s and their generally bad overall condition the Il-10s, were quickly withdrawn from service.

In October of 1958 it was decided to ferry fifty of the B-33s that were in the best condition to Craiova Air Base where they were stored in hangars. In June of 1960, Romanian military aviation was reorganized, and it was decided to withdraw the remaining B-33 from active service and replace them with MiG-15s.

In 1957, twenty-four crated B-33s and CB-33s were delivered the Czech Air Force to the Kingdom of Yemen, which became the Yemen Arab Republic (North Yemen) during 1962. The aircraft were delivered without armament to Yemen and were reassembled by Czech specialists. Besides the B-33 and the CB-33, the Czech government also delivered a number of Zlin Z-126 and Yakovlev Yak-11 trainers to Yemen.